How to Get a Job and
and
◆ Keep It ◆

SECOND EDITION

How to Get a Job and -Keep It-

Career and Life Skills You Need to Succeed

SECOND EDITION

SUSAN MOREM

Ferguson
An imprint of Infobase Publishing

How to Get A Job and Keep It, Second Edition

Copyright © 2007, 2002 by Sue Morem

Ferguson
An imprint of Infobase Publishing
132 West 31st Street
New York, NY 10001

ISBN-10: 0-8160-6775-9
ISBN-13: 978-0-8160-6775-6

Library of Congress Cataloging-in-Publication Data

Morem, Susan.
  How to get a job and keep it : career and life skills you need to succeed / Susan Morem.—2nd ed.
      p. cm.
  Includes index.
  ISBN 0-8160-6775-9 (hc : alk. paper)
  1. Job hunting. 2. Résumés (Employment) 3. Vocational guidance. 4. Career development. I. Title.
  HF5382.7.M645 2007
  650.14—dc22   2006030645

Ferguson books are available at special discounts when purchased in bulk quantities for businesses, associations, institutions, or sales promotions. Please call our Special Sales Department in New York at (212) 967-8800 or (800) 322-8755.

You can find Ferguson on the World Wide Web at http://www.fergpubco.com

Text design by Mary Susan Ryan-Flynn
Cover design by Salvatore Luongo

Printed in the United States of America

MP MSRF 10 9 8 7 6 5 4 3 2 1

This book is printed on acid-free paper.

◆

To my husband Steve and my three daughters
Stephanie, Stacie, and Samantha: You inspire me.
This book is dedicated to each one of you.

◆

CONTENTS

Acknowledgments ix

Introduction xi

Chapter 1: Myths and Truths of Success 1

Chapter 2: The First Step: Getting to Know Yourself 7

**Chapter 3: Gain Experience and Knowledge Through
Internships and Informational Interviews** 21

Chapter 4: The Job of Finding a Job 27

Chapter 5: Finding the Job You Want 39

Chapter 6: Putting Yourself on Paper 49

Chapter 7: Prepare for Interview Success 61

Chapter 8: Dressing for Interview and Career Success . . . 71

Chapter 9: Do's and Don'ts of Interviewing 95

Chapter 10: The Interview Is Over: Now What? 113

Chapter 11: When You're the Newcomer 121

**Chapter 12: Communication Skills That Work at
Getting and Keeping Work** 133

Chapter 13: Habits of Successful People 149

Chapter 14: Getting Along with Others 163

Chapter 15: Avoiding Potential Pitfalls 181

**Chapter 16: When You're Disappointed
and Disillusioned** 191

Further Reading Resources 203

Index 207

ACKNOWLEDGMENTS

This book would not have been possible without the input of many people. A big thanks to everyone who contributed to the first edition and the second, including those of you who responded to surveys, shared your experiences and stories, and those who took the time to review the book and comment. Thank you, James Chambers for planting the idea of a second edition and for your ongoing support of my work. I can't tell you how much I value your input and appreciate you as an editor. A special thanks to Petra Marquart, for sharing your insight and encouraging me to write the first edition of this book.

INTRODUCTION

My daughter Stacie, who was 15 at the time, had just started a summer job when I received a call early one morning from her boss, wondering why she wasn't at work. Assuming she had overslept, I woke her only to discover she had no intention of getting up and going to work. She informed me she was planning on taking the day off so she could say good-bye to her friends who were going away for the summer.

I asked Stacie if she had permission to take the day off, and she told me she assumed she did because she left a voice message telling her boss that she wouldn't be coming to work that day. I was stunned. "You *told* your boss you were taking the day off instead of *asking*?" I shrieked. She didn't understand why I was so upset, and I didn't understand how she could be so irresponsible. Yet she thought she *was* being responsible by calling to say she wasn't coming to work that day.

A jumble of thoughts raced through my head: *What was she thinking? How could saying good-bye to friends be more important to her than going to work? Didn't she understand people were depending on her?*

This incident was a defining moment for me. I had sensed that young workers needed the information in this book, and now my hunch had been confirmed. My daughter would never purposely upset her boss. She just didn't know what was expected. I began to think about all of the assumptions she and other young and first-time employees make about their jobs and responsibilities. I thought about all of the mistakes that could be avoided if only they understood the expectations of their employers. I decided I could do something to help.

I began speaking with companies to learn more about the challenges they face when working with young professionals. I talked with young adults to learn about their concerns and to determine how prepared they were for the business world. My goal: to provide young people, via this book, with the information they need to know as they enter the workplace and begin building their careers.

As a young adult entering the workforce, you are savvy and, in many ways far ahead of young adults from previous generations. From a young age, you've been exposed to the Internet, voicemail, e-mail, buddy lists, television, PG, PG-13- and R-rated movies, and more. All of this exposure forces you to grow up very quickly. You may be very independent and accustomed to fending for yourself due to the long working hours of your parents. Maybe you've had a taste of adulthood while growing up. Now, think about your perceptions about work. Where have they come from? Whatever experiences, education, or training you have had to prepare you, when you enter the business world you most likely will discover that it is very different from the world you are used to living in. The more realistic you are, the easier the transition will be.

When you understand what it takes to get and keep a job, everyone benefits. This book is written for you, the job seeker, and for the people you work for and with. The information can help you achieve your goals and eliminate obstacles that could get in your way. Opportunities are out there and await you—it's up to you to find or create them.

I wish you much success and joy in your career and in life.

—*Sue Morem*

Chapter 1

Myths and Truths of Success

Most people start out wanting to succeed, hoping for a bright future. Yet, how many achieve the success they seek? If knowledge is power—and I believe it is—then *knowing* what is expected is crucial to your success. How can you know? By observing and asking questions.

People hold varying philosophies about success. You've probably heard a number of the many clichés out there: "No pain, no gain"; "It's not what you know, it's who you know"; "If at first you don't succeed, try again"; "When the going gets tough, the tough get going"; and a host of others. Some of the things people tell you can be motivating, but don't believe everything you hear. Some of it may be misleading.

To be clear about what is expected, you must sift through the myths and truths of success—both yours and others. The following truths about many common myths will help you get into the right frame of mind.

MYTH: WORK HARD AND YOU'LL SUCCEED.

Success is difficult to achieve without some hard work involved; however, plenty of people who work hard are not as successful as they'd like to be. While hard work is important, success comes from much more. You can work long hours and feel exhausted at the end of each day, but chances are you won't feel successful if that is all you do.

Success comes in many forms. One way to measure your success is to identify specific goals you want to achieve and then work toward meeting them. Once you are working, you will also need to understand your employer's goals and objectives and work toward meeting those as well.

Hard work is an important component of success, but not the only one. Your success, or lack of it, is the result of so much more.

You will discover as you read this book that *who you are* is as important as what you do.

The most successful people understand the importance of combining hard work with the right attitude, good people skills, a willingness to learn, change, and a desire to contribute. Strive to find joy and meaning in what you do. When you enjoy going to work each day you won't even realize how hard you are working!

MYTH: SUCCESS IN SCHOOL GUARANTEES SUCCESS IN WORK.

Many people believe that if they've been successful academically they will succeed in a job, but your career success is dependent on many additional factors. It is important to understand the difference between what it takes to succeed in school and what you need to do to excel in the workplace.

In school, if you miss a day of classes, you can find out what you missed and make up the work. If you are a part of a group, everyone is affected, but if not, the only person your absence affects is you. When you are employed and you miss a day of work, you may not be able to make up what you missed. Your absence affects those you work with and could affect your employer's business. The business world is fast paced. Your contribution, and everyone else's—from entry-level clerk to company CEO—is important. People are counting on you.

MYTH: SKILL AND KNOWLEDGE ARE THE KEYS TO SUCCESS.

There is far more to a job than just showing up and completing your work. Employers expect you to show up every day on time, looking good, enthused, and focused on the job at hand. As basic as these expectations sound, it isn't easy for many people to show up consistently in this manner. The people who do, however, have an advantage.

I've never heard of anyone criticized for being too positive or too professional, but I've heard a lot of criticism about people who are negative, unreliable, and difficult to get along with. You will have an advantage in the workplace and in life if you are dependable, professional, flexible, and likeable.

MYTH: DOING A JOB WELL WILL BRING SUCCESS.

Doing a job well is a key factor for success, but your ability to succeed encompasses much more. Don't overlook the importance of your attitude and demeanor; picking up after yourself, pitching in without being asked, and being consistent in all of your behaviors. There are many unspoken expectations in the workplace—unspoken because employers assume you know what they want. When you don't know what is expected, you are the one who suffers. Many managers and supervisors will not address the little nuances of employee performance, and will pay attention only to the serious issues or offenses. However, it is often the little things that get in the way of a person's success.

MYTH: MOST PEOPLE FIND A JOB WITHIN THE FIRST MONTH OF LOOKING.

If you're like most people, you will be excited at the start of your job search. However, if you are expecting to find a job right away, within the first month or two of looking, you may be setting yourself up for disappointment. Typically, the process takes much longer. Two to three months are average, but many people wait six months or more before getting the kind of offer they want to accept.

Looking for a job can—and should be—a full-time job in itself. It's tempting to use your newfound free time to relax and do as you please, but be prepared for an extended, never-ending job search if you do.

You may tire of filling out applications, going on interviews, and waiting for a response, but keep doing these things and more. Treat looking for a job like a job by devoting ample time to your job search activities every day.

MYTH: EMPLOYERS LOOK TO HIRE THOSE WITH THE HIGHEST GRADE POINT AVERAGE.

If you wonder how your grade point average or the school you went to will affect your chances of getting a job, you may be focusing on the wrong things. Attending a top school and doing well academically are assets, but no guarantee your job search will be any easier.

You may be terrific at taking tests, but it doesn't demonstrate your ability to communicate effectively or work well with others, which is also important to employers. The results of a CollegeGrad.com survey to determine what employers want most when hiring new college grads found 37 percent of employers ranked a student's major as the top priority for hiring consideration. Also very important to employers were the students' interviewing skills and their internships or experience.

When you are interviewing for a job, you need to offer more than your school smarts. You need to be *business smart* as well.

MYTH: MOST JOBS ARE FOUND THROUGH ADVERTISEMENTS.

A job search is a complicated process and must be carried out methodically. Many job seekers rely on job postings and advertisements to find a job. This is a mistake. Research has found that many, if not most, job openings are *never* advertised.

It is estimated that 80 percent of all professional jobs are filled through personal contacts and networking. This doesn't mean you shouldn't read the want ads, but if you want to increase your chances of finding a job, you need to do more than scan ads. There are many available resources to use, with your personal contacts being one of the best resources.

MYTH: SOME PEOPLE ARE LUCKIER THAN OTHERS AND THEREFORE MORE SUCCESSFUL.

Rarely is success due to luck. Although some people appear to have lucky breaks, if you take the time to look at why these people seem lucky, you will see it isn't due to luck at all. "Lucky" people create their own good fortune, which doesn't come to them as they sit passively and wait. They are actively creating and going after their goals and the success they seek.

You can do many things to increase your chances of success. Many of them are included in this book. But ultimately, your success—or lack of it—is up to *you*, not luck.

MYTH: SUCCESS IS COMPLICATED AND DIFFICULT TO ACHIEVE.

You probably will breathe a sigh of relief when you are finally offered a job. You may even assume that once you are hired you can let your guard down, but beware: everything you do or don't do will impact your salary and your advancement opportunities. However, success isn't as complicated or difficult to achieve as you think.

Decide now what success means to you. Identify all the things you must do to achieve your goals, then do those things.

Stay true to yourself and be yourself because *you* are the difference. It can take years to get where you want to be. Be patient—and be persistent. Look around and you will see that *anything* is possible.

Chapter 2

The First Step: Getting to Know Yourself

DECIDING WHAT YOU WANT TO DO

I was invited to speak to a group of 20 high school seniors who were part of an experimental business preparation class. Before I began, everyone had a chance to introduce him- or herself and tell me what they planned to do with their futures. "I'm going into interior design," one young woman responded. "Entertainment," the next person said. It went on: sports management, marketing, theater. Every person in attendance knew what he or she wanted to pursue. I was amazed and impressed that these 17- and 18-year-olds knew exactly what they wanted to do in their professional lives. When I was a senior in high school, if you asked me what I was striving for, my answer would have been, "To graduate!"

You may or may not yet know what you want to do with your life. At some point you will have to make that decision, but if you don't know yet, don't despair. Perhaps you are the type who likes to see where life takes you. Or maybe you have an idea but aren't really sure what to do with it. Whatever stage of discovery you are in, you've got plenty of time and more resources than ever before available to find and discover what is out there for you.

Choosing a career is one of the most important decisions you will make and is not something to be decided on a whim. If you aren't sure what you want to do, this is the time to discover all that is out there for you and, in the process, learn more about yourself. You want to ensure you make the right choice when you accept a job.

Looking for a job, especially a first job, can be trying. You're likely to have highs and lows, so anticipate them, but whatever you do, don't give up. You *will* find a job. You just have to keep searching until you find the job that fits enough of your criteria to be a good job for you. Chances are you will be rejected before you are accepted. Keep in mind that it isn't you, personally, that is being rejected. It may have more to do with the job requirements, the level of training or experience required, or the fact that someone else was a better fit for a particular position. When you don't get a job you really want, the odds are good that a better opportunity is yet to come.

Take charge of your career. Accepting a job isn't a lifelong commitment, but the decision shouldn't be made too lightly. You may be tempted to accept the first offer that comes along or the job that offers you the most money, but you will be much happier if you can find a job that offers you at least some of what you are looking for in a position.

DEFINING YOUR FIRST JOB

As you begin your quest to find your first job, I am willing to bet this isn't your *first* job at all. How would you respond to the following questions?

- Did you ever work a summer job?
- Have you ever earned an allowance? What did you do to earn it?
- Did you ever mow lawns or babysit for neighbors when you were young?
- Have you ever held a part- or full-time job?

If you answered yes to any of these questions, then it is likely you've had a number of jobs. Before you dismiss your previous work experience or assume that mowing lawns or babysitting doesn't count as a real job, take some time to evaluate what you've learned from all of your experiences thus far. Start by listing all of the jobs you've ever held. Then, ask yourself the following questions:

- What did I like best about my previous job(s)?

- What did I like least?

- What specific tasks did I perform?

- What was I really good at?

- What were some of the biggest challenges I faced, and how did I overcome them?

- What would I do differently today as a result of what I've learned?

- How did this experience impact me?

Spend some time answering these questions. You might want to write down your responses on a sheet of paper in order to help you organize your thoughts. The time you take to do this will pay off. For example, when asked about a previous job in an interview, rather than saying, "I mowed lawns for my neighbors," think about all of the other aspects of what you did, emphasizing those that are unique.

My neighbor Blair not only mowed lawns as a young adult, but he found ways to do more, including aerating lawns in the spring and shoveling driveways and sidewalks in the winter. He was always looking for ways to grow his lawn care "business" and provide new services to his customers.

Tina, a childhood friend, not only babysat for a family for years, but she also did some filing for her employer's home business, too. Did you just babysit or mow lawns, or was there more to what you did?

Imagine an employer hearing a response like this: "I managed a lawn care service for four years. Each spring I made personal visits to over 40 houses in my neighborhood to solicit their yard business and determine their needs. As the business grew, I hired others to assist me and gained experience in managing people. In addition, with so many homeowners working outside the home, I discovered that invoicing them was the best method of collecting payment. I created an invoicing program on my computer to facilitate billing. Overall, in addition to mowing lawns, I gained experience in running a small business." That's quite a different response than simply saying, "I mowed lawns for my neighbors."

It is important to identify the skills you've gained and transfer them to the job for which you are applying. Look beyond the duties you performed and think about the accomplishments you made and what you learned as a result.

YOUR PAST CAN LEAD TO FUTURE OPPORTUNITIES

Everything you have done or accomplished up to this point will help you as you begin to define yourself for prospective employers. Think about your answers to the following questions:

- What volunteer work have I done?
- Am I or have I been involved in any school or outside organizations?
- What leadership positions have I held?
- What awards or special recognition have I received?
- What hobbies do I have?
- What skills do I utilize in my leisure time?

An experience doesn't have to pay you money or be career related for it to have value and impact. Spend some time thinking about all of your accomplishments and what you've gained and learned.

Perhaps you've had a challenging experience. You might talk about how you dealt with it and what you learned as a result. When my sister Eileen was 15, she accepted a job as a nanny for a family in our neighborhood. One day, the mother, who was going through a divorce and was depressed, overdosed on her medication. She pushed a dresser against her door so no one could get in. When she told my sister what she had done, my sister immediately called our home to tell my mother to come over, called an ambulance, and took the children out of the house. If Eileen were asked in an interview to relate a challenging experience and how she reacted to it, what might she say based on this incident? Think about it. She was dealing with life and death. She had to act fast, think on her feet, remain calm, and protect the young children. Eileen demonstrated her ability to react quickly and think clearly under pressure. In addition, after the incident, she told the woman that she wouldn't babysit for her anymore if she ever did anything like that again—showing that she was able and willing to set boundaries.

When I was 18, a friend of mine invited me to a cosmetics demonstration that she hosted in her home. We sat around her dining room table, and Bonnie, an attractive young woman who was a beauty consultant, showed us how to properly cleanse our faces and apply makeup. It was an enjoyable experience, and since I had never had any prior makeup lessons, I learned lots of new tips.

At the end of the event, Bonnie recruited me to become a consultant and conduct the demonstrations myself. She thought I had all of the necessary ingredients to be successful as a beauty consultant, and I was both flattered and excited at this unique business opportunity.

I took out my first business loan and asked my family and friends to hold events for me. I also started using the skin care regime. To my horror, within a few weeks, I began to break out with a terrible case of acne. I called Bonnie and asked for advice. She didn't seem too surprised about my problem and told me that the product was working because it was removing the impurities in my skin.

As far as I was concerned, the impurities could stay in my skin. I looked awful and was worried about making claims that this product could improve the skin. Anyone who looked at me would see the contradiction. If the skin care regime worked so well, why didn't it work on my skin? I knew that there was no way I could stand before prospective buyers and make claims that they would have beautiful skin when, by taking one look at me, they would know I was lying. No one would want to go through what I did to have nice skin. I got out of the beauty consulting business as fast as I got in.

I learned some important lasting lessons that have become the basis for what I speak and write about today. I instinctively knew that I could not sell a skin care product and promise people beautiful skin with my skin in terrible condition. My message would be confusing since my skin didn't reflect what I was promising, and people wouldn't trust me as a result. That was the biggest lesson, but I learned much more about starting a business, recruiting people to become consultants, calling people to host events for me, selling a product, and setting up a business and office. I kept thinking about my experiences and the lessons I learned until I was satisfied that I had skills that would help me sell myself to a prospective employer. The more you understand yourself the easier it is to convey who you are to others.

SELL YOURSELF

Regardless of your chosen career field and whether you consider yourself a salesperson or not, when you are a job seeker, you are a salesperson. When you are interviewing for a job, you need to sell yourself as the best person for the job. Make sure you are selling yourself effectively.

Pay attention to the words you use when describing yourself. Do you speak favorably of yourself and your accomplishments? Every word you use when you talk about yourself paints a picture of who you are in the minds of others. To effectively sell yourself, you must know yourself. Take some time to think about and respond to the following questions:

- What words best describe you?

- What are your finest qualities?

- What areas do you need to improve upon?

- What accomplishments are you most proud of?

- How do your friends describe you?

- How does your family describe you?

- How would a previous employer describe you?

- How would one of your teachers describe you?

- Why should someone hire you?

Spend time thinking about and practicing your responses to these questions. Be prepared to talk about yourself positively and enthusiastically to the people with whom you meet, network, and interview. In addition, know what skills you possess and be willing to talk about them. Don't assume others know your strengths or skills and don't underestimate or take your unique qualities for granted.

Peter Vogt, a career counselor, the Campus Career Coach for Monster.com, and author of Career Wisdom for College Students, says that many new graduates take their computer skills for granted and don't realize, for example, that the ability to do research on the Internet is a marketable attribute. They think that "everyone can do that" because their only points of reference are their fellow students. Vogt says that many people in the business world don't possess this strength. It's important to play up your computer skills if you have them and to continuously learn new ones.

WORDS CAN MAKE A DIFFERENCE

Think carefully about the words you use when describing yourself and your accomplishments. Choosing just the right words helps you provide an accurate portrayal of your skills and background. Being succinct and precise lets you get the most out of your presentation on paper and in person.

Next, look at the words you chose and cross off any you believe are unflattering characteristics—words that you would want to avoid using in an interview or in the workplace when describing yourself. Then read through the list again, and this time make a note on a

separate piece of paper (or using a different color pen) of the words
that you think are valuable traits of successful people.

As you read the following words, note on a separate sheet of paper
those that describe you best:

Accurate	Extroverted	Organized
Achiever	Flexible	Original
Aggressive	Forceful	Outgoing
Approachable	Friendly	Outspoken
Arrogant	Gentle	Polite
Assertive	Gracious	Positive
Committed	Humble	Precise
Competitive	Impatient	Receptive
Confident	Independent	Reserved
Considerate	Influential	Respectful
Controlling	Intellectual	Restless
Creative	Intelligent	Restrained
Daring	Introverted	Sarcastic
Dedicated	Intuitive	Self-centered
Dependable	Leader	Self-reliant
Determined	Loyal	Soft-spoken
Diplomatic	Motivated	Supportive
Disciplined	Naive	Tactful
Dynamic	Negative	Team player
Energetic	Obedient	Tolerant
Enthusiastic	Open-minded	Trustworthy
Entrepreneurial	Optimistic	Versatile

Now compare the two lists. Which traits did you choose in the
second list (your perception of successful people) that you didn't

select in the first list (your perception of yourself)? What can you do to develop these successful traits?

It is important to see yourself as you want to be seen and to incorporate words representing the traits you desire into your vocabulary. You will be selling your skills and qualities. Choose your words carefully as you speak about yourself so you convey the right message.

KNOW WHAT YOU WANT AND WHAT YOU'LL SETTLE FOR

There are unique circumstances surrounding the search for a first job. You may or may not know exactly what you need or want from a job. Other than receiving a paycheck and utilizing your knowledge and skills in your chosen field, you may become confused as you view all of your job options. Think very carefully about the kind of job you want. Although you may be motivated by salary, don't let money be the only reason you accept a job. I know of many people who earn large amounts of money who are not necessarily happy. Money is not the only way to have a happy life. Happiness is a choice that comes as a result of making the right decisions. If you happen to earn a good living doing the things that make you happy, so much the better.

When you work full time, you spend, on average, 40 hours a week at your job. You spend more time working than doing anything else, except maybe sleeping. You may as well spend your time doing something you enjoy.

People who work full time crave balance in their lives. You undoubtedly have developed interests and hobbies over the years. You shouldn't have to give up everything you love doing because you work full time, but you might be surprised at how little free time you have and how precious it becomes. You will want to find a job that enables you to have balance in your life and to pursue those things that are most important to you.

You might have an idea of your ideal job, but be realistic about what you will or won't accept. There are many factors to consider that go beyond a job description and duties when looking for a job or accepting an offer. A few things to consider:

Location

Are you willing to relocate? Have you thought about what it would be like to move to a new city? Some people love the experience, while others are surprised at how much they miss their family and friends. It takes time to adjust to working full time at a new job, but it can take even more time adjusting to the unfamiliar, whether it's living on your own or simply realizing how alone you are.

Have you thought about the amount of time you are willing to spend commuting to and from work each day? If you take public transportation, your commute can be a time to read or relax. If you will be driving to and from work each day and have a long commute, you need to not only consider the time you will spend commuting, but the costs you will incur through the price of gas and the wear and tear on your car.

You might find the perfect job, but if the location is too far from home, the town too small, or the weather unbearable, you might decide the job isn't so perfect after all. It's good to be open and flexible, but be realistic, too; think long and hard about where you want to work and the location where you'd be happiest.

Salary and Benefits

If you are looking for your first full-time job, an annual salary may seem like a lot of money. Once taxes are taken out and you pay your living expenses and bills, you may find out it isn't so much after all. Have you thought about how much money you need to make? Are you willing to start at a lower salary in order to gain experience and eventually move into a position with a higher salary? Have you thought about the benefits you want? Don't overlook benefits or forget to consider their value as part of your compensation. You may not pay too much attention to your health plan if you are young and healthy, but should you become ill you don't want to be without good coverage. Only you can decide what you need for salary and benefits and what you will accept, and it's best to think about these things in advance, before you accept a job.

Hours

Are you expecting set hours? Depending on the job, you may be expected to work more than 40 hours a week. Are you willing to work unusual hours: overtime, evenings, weekends, or on holidays? Know what kind of work schedule will work best for you and be aware of the lifestyle changes you'll have to make to accommodate your new schedule.

I met a young intern at a television station in New York City when I was doing a book tour. As he escorted me to the studio his exhaustion was obvious. Upon my questioning him, he told me that he was having a tough time adjusting to his new work hours, which began in the wee hours of the morning. His work schedule was affecting his social life because he had to be in bed early each night in order to get up for work at 4:00 A.M. He had never thought about the impact this type of schedule would have on him. Be sure you think about your lifestyle and the changes you may need to make due to the hours you will be working.

Environment/Culture

It is important to know what type of environment you will be working in and that you understand and are comfortable with the culture of an organization before you decide to work there. An organization's culture is like a code of conduct, determining which behavior is acceptable and which is not. Cultures will vary from company to company. You can gather information about the culture of an organization by doing research, observing, talking with others who work there, and by reading its mission statement and other written materials.

Early on in my career I worked for six months in an organization whose culture made me most uncomfortable. The sales group, which I was a part of, was very close. They frequently went out after work and partied on the weekend. They teased each other, hugged each other, and acted in a manner that made me feel awkward and uncomfortable. I left after six months because I knew I didn't fit in.

Ask yourself, what is the atmosphere like; is it more formal or informal? Do employees seem happy? What is the mission statement; does it resonate with you? Is there a lot of socializing? Is after-hours socializing, volunteering, etc. encouraged, or even expected?

Gather as much information as you can about an organization and pay close attention to how you feel when you are there to help you determine if it is an environment you will be comfortable working in.

There are a number of additional factors to consider; some may be more important to you than others. Know what matters most to you and what you can live with and without. Be clear about what you want, but be flexible and open to the opportunities presented to you. The clearer you are about what you want and why you are drawn to the type of work you have chosen, the easier it will be for you to communicate that knowledge to others. Identify the type of work you'd prefer to do, the kind of environment you'd like to work in, and the tasks you'd enjoy doing most, but don't cling to an unrealistic vision of a job that may not exist.

Whatever you do, don't compare yourself to others. Some of your peers will secure a job before they graduate. Some will find a job quickly and others may experience a longer search. Everyone's path is different. Consider that wherever you are is where you need to be.

SUMMARY

Remember

- ✔ Choosing a career is an important decision that should not be taken lightly. If you aren't sure about what you want to do, take some time to explore the many options available to you.

- ✔ Get to know yourself. Think about your strengths and weaknesses, your likes and dislikes. The more you know about you, the easier it will be for others to get to know you too.

✔ Define your job search objectives. Think about the direction of your career. Know what you will and won't accept.

✔ Discover what you've gained from your work experience. Evaluate every job you've held and identify what you learned as a result. Be prepared to talk about this in interviews.

✔ Identify the words that define who you are. Recognize your strengths and your weaknesses. Know who you are and who you want to be.

✔ Put on your selling shoes. You are the product, and you need to sell yourself to potential employers. No one can sell you as well as you can sell yourself.

Chapter 3

Gain Experience and Knowledge Through Internships and Informational Interviews

INFORMATIONAL INTERVIEWS

One of the best ways to learn more about a company, industry, or occupation is by talking with people who know firsthand what it is like. What better way to learn about a career than to talk to those who are already working in the field? It's a great way to meet people and learn about companies you may want to work for.

Conducting informational interviews can be useful while you are still in school or when you are looking for a job. Informational interviews can help you early on when you are making decisions about your career, when you want to learn more about what's expected, when you need some advice, or when you are starting your job search.

An informational interview can either reinforce your career goals or cause you to rethink your plan. It is different than a job interview because the purpose of this type of meeting is to gather information. It is less stressful than a job interview because the tables are turned; you are the one doing the interviewing. Informational interviews can help you:

- Make valuable connections and expand your network
- Practice your interviewing skills and increase your confidence
- Grasp the reality of what a particular job entails
- Gain knowledge and insight about a company or industry

- Ask questions you might not feel comfortable asking in a typical interview

- Uncover additional resources and opportunities available to you

- Make important decisions about your future

- Enable you to talk about industry-specific issues, and better prepare you for a job interview

The purpose of an informational interview is to obtain information, not a job. However, informational interviews do help generate referrals and occasionally, may lead to a job offer.

Jay Lipe, author of *The Marketing Toolkit for Growing Businesses* (Chammerson Press, LLC, 2002), recalls scheduling an informational interview that led to an offer. As a standard practice during his job search, Jay scheduled informational interviews with individuals in fields that he wanted to learn more about. Let me emphasize that Jay's intent with these informational interviews was *not* to get a job. Rather, it was to learn from respected leaders about certain fields. During one of these informational interviews, he met with the marketing manager of a real estate firm. After the informational interview was over, he thanked the contact for the information she provided and went on his merry way. One week later, he received a phone call from that same marketing manager who informed him she was leaving her job for another and asked Jay if he was interested in taking her job.

There likely were other, more qualified and experienced candidates deserving of the offer, but it was Jay who came to mind because of his recent visit. Flattered as he was, he declined the offer. Because of the informational interview, he had gained a clearer understanding of what he wanted and had determined he did not want to pursue a career in real estate.

Don't rely on informational interviews for finding a job, but do recognize the value of conducting them and in connecting with others. Every time you talk with someone on the phone or in person, you remind that person about you, increasing the chance that person will think of you when opportunities arise.

If you are lucky enough to be connected with someone who works in your desired field, call and ask for an informational interview. If you don't have any contacts in your industry of interest but are hoping to obtain an informational interview, call the human resources department of a company in that field and ask to be connected with someone who can help you. If the thought of calling a stranger to ask for help seems strange, don't let it stop you. There is always a chance you may be turned down, but you might be surprised at how many people are willing to help you.

When you have an appointment for an informational interview, treat it as you would any other type of interview. Wear appropriate attire, arrive on time, and be prepared. It will help if you bring a list of questions to ask. Think about the things you want to know. This type of interview enables you to find out about a typical day on the job, what the person enjoys or dislikes, and much more. Some questions you might ask are:

- How did you get into this line of work?

- What experience and requirements are needed to work in and be successful this field?

- When hiring, what do you look for in job candidates?

- What's the best way to break into this field or industry?

- What is a typical day like?

- What sets your company apart from the competition?

- What can you tell me about the corporate culture?

- How do you typically post job openings or find people to work here?

You don't want to overstay your welcome—informational interviews should be brief. The people you interview with are busy people and you will be taking precious time away from their work. Determine how much time the person has and stay within that time frame. Keep your informational interview to a half hour or less.

When the interview is over, thank the person for his or her time, leave your resume or card, and get a business card. After the interview, do what you would after any other interview; make notes about the interview and anything you need to follow up on, then write and send a thank you note.

INTERNSHIPS

If you are wondering if you should participate in an internship, the answer is yes. It is one of the best ways to gain relevant career experience and become better prepared for work in your chosen field. Typically, an internship is brief and considered a temporary period of employment with a company. Some internship programs are structured; others are much more laid back.

Some companies pay their interns; others do not. An internship has value, however, whether you earn a salary or do the work for free. Some internship opportunities are better than others, but no internship is a waste of time. Any time you are a part of the inner workings of a business or office you will benefit by both observing and being involved.

An internship is no longer a "choice" or an "elective" for college students. It has basically become a requirement, according to Peter Vogt, who has this to say: "From an employer's perspective, a college student or new graduate who relies solely on his or her education is someone to be passed over for another student/graduate who has supplemented his or her education with practical, real-world experience(s). Companies and organizations have too much to do and too little time and money to invest in teaching you what you should have learned, in their opinion, in college."

The best time to seek an internship is while you are still in school; however, it's never too late to pursue an internship experience. Some people wait until after graduation, others intern when exploring new areas of interest. Internships have many benefits and help you to:

- Gain career-related experience

- Determine the type of work you enjoy and want to pursue

- Make valuable contacts and connections
- Get your foot in the door at a company, possibly leading to future employment
- Understand the dynamics of a work environment
- Acquire new skills and abilities
- Learn about an industry and make informed decisions about your career path
- Put into practice what you have learned
- Generate work-related references

BENEFITING FROM EXPERIENCE

You don't have to wait until you have a degree to get experience, and if you do, you may be at a disadvantage. In a 2000 survey developed by Office Team, an administrative staffing service, 47 percent of executives polled rated professional experience as the most important quality in hiring new graduates, even more than the type of degree earned (18 percent) or grade point average (17 percent). Working as an intern or in a temporary position allows you to build your skills and business network and enhance your marketability to prospective employers.

You can go about finding an internship in much the same way you would go about finding a job. Search the Internet, utilize your career center, contact companies, and network with others. Many students intern during the summer, however, you will find internship positions are available year-round.

Think of an internship as a job. You'll need to send out your resume and go on interviews, so prepare as you would for a job interview and practice interviewing so that you will present yourself well.

Make the most out of your internship by viewing it as a real job in which you must perform well, whether you are paid or not. Be open to learning and to the ideas of others. Ask questions, offer to assist others, and do what you can to be a model employee. You may want to use some of the people you work with as references, so make sure you leave a positive impression with everyone you meet.

SUMMARY

Remember

- ✔ Conduct informational interviews to help you learn more about what it takes to succeed in your given field.

- ✔ Informational interviews enable you to ask intelligent questions when interviewing for a job.

- ✔ Don't let your fear of calling someone you don't know get in your way. Most people will empathize with you and do what they can to help you.

- ✔ Gain experience through an internship opportunity. An internship can help you overcome a lack of experience and can help you to get your foot in the door of an organization.

- ✔ Prepare for an informational interview or internship interview as you would for a job interview. Research the company, make a list of questions to ask, know who you will be meeting with, be on time, and send a thank you note after the interview is over.

Chapter 4

The Job of Finding a Job

ANY JOB WORTH HAVING IS WORTH PURSUING

For some people, looking for a job is a thrilling adventure; for others, it is a daunting undertaking. I was excited about my first real job search. By the time I made the decision to leave school I was convinced I would make a better salesperson than student. It had been a difficult decision to make. Part of me wanted to stay in school, but another part of me longed to get out into the real world and put some of the knowledge I had gained to use. I read every self-help book I could get my hands on. And after taking the Dale Carnegie course from Dale Carnegie Training, an internationally renowned corporate training company, I began my job search.

I worked part time waiting on tables and spent the rest of my time looking for a job in sales. I enthusiastically responded to ads, but after a few weeks had gone by without a job offer, I became concerned. When I realized that finding a job could take months, not weeks, I was disillusioned. But I kept looking.

I began my job search by reading the want ads in the newspaper. Most of the positions advertised required someone who either had experience or a college degree. I didn't have either, but that didn't stop me from responding to ads that sounded intriguing. Fortunately my resume and cover letter triggered some interest, and I was called for interviews. Although I lacked some of the credentials these companies were looking for, I must have done something right in the interviews because I was asked back for second and third interviews.

Jim, a sales manager with a Fortune 500 company and one of the interviewers, told me that although I didn't have everything they were looking for in a candidate, I did have something special. "You know," he said, "I really think you would be great in this position.

You're personable. You have a positive attitude, and lots of enthusiasm. Why don't you go get some sales experience under your belt and come back in a year?"

I was thrilled by his confidence in my ability, but had a difficult time understanding why he wouldn't hire me and give me a chance to prove myself. I wanted to jump-start my career right then—not a year down the road. Yet I heard the same thing repeatedly. Everyone I met agreed I would succeed in sales, and they all liked my confidence and my enthusiasm, but no one was willing to take a chance on me.

I began to dread Sundays. The newspaper would arrive with the new job listings in the employment section, and my search would begin all over again. All of the ads that sounded too good to be true were too good to be true. I could have found a job if I were willing to invest money or to work strictly on commission. But that wasn't what I wanted. I wanted a job with a regular paycheck. The jobs that didn't require experience did require a monetary investment, which I couldn't make. I was losing momentum, my belief in myself, and, worst of all, I was losing what everyone said they liked best about me—my enthusiasm.

We all have to start somewhere, yet when employers want to hire those with experience, it becomes a vicious cycle. I kept asking myself: how do I get experience if I can't get a job?

One way to gain experience is by participating in an internship program (discussed in Chapter 3). If you are able to acquire an internship, go for it, but if you can't, don't despair; seek opportunities for the experience you need and continue to work with the experience you have.

I was relieved when I finally got the break I needed, which was the result of some volunteer work I had been doing with the Dale Carnegie courses. Upon discovering that I was interested in a sales job, the people at Dale Carnegie offered me a position selling their training courses.

I will always appreciate that opportunity. I was on a straight commission, which meant I only made money when I sold something. Although I would have preferred a job with some financial guarantee, I needed experience and realized I had to give something to gain something.

After working for Dale Carnegie for about a year, I contacted Jim at the Fortune 500 company that had been interested in me one year prior. I told him that I was still interested in working for him and that I now had the sales experience he sought. I got the job and a chance to prove myself in the big leagues.

Jim could have easily forgotten me, and perhaps he did, but I didn't forget him. I knew he was impressed when I came back a year later. *Any job worth having is worth pursuing.* Don't expect to sit back and wait for the phone to ring, because it won't. You need to go out and make things happen. You will feel a greater sense of control and get what you want much faster.

FINDING A JOB *IS* A JOB

The process involved in finding a job is like having a job; you must devote ample time to your search and work hard to find the job you want. You need to be prepared, committed, and resourceful. And, above all, if you want to stand out and obtain extraordinary results you need to be extraordinary.

Looking for a job is similar to starting your own business. You are in the business of finding a job. If you were to start your own business, you would need a place to run it and the tools to work effectively. Do you have a place to conduct your job search and the equipment you need to do your job?

The following are some of the typical items necessary to run a business (or job search) effectively:

- Telephone

- Answering machine/voicemail

- Fax machine

- Computer

- Printer

- Internet connection

- Stationery and envelopes

- Calendar/date book

- Pens, pencils

- Postage

- Business cards/copies of resume

Some of these tools are essential, while others are optional. If you don't have all of the equipment you need, as long as you have access to what you need (via a library, career center, friend, etc.), you will manage just fine.

ESTABLISH A ROUTINE

If you are unemployed and out of school, you will have a lot of time on your hands. This may be a welcome relief at first if you've been on a hectic schedule, but over time don't be surprised if you discover you miss having someplace to go. Too many empty days can lead to a feeling of isolation and lack of productivity.

Consider yourself self-employed; no one is going to monitor your work or tell you what to do. You can work a little each day or work a lot; it's up to you. If you choose to sleep until noon, it is your choice, but not the best choice if you are serious about finding a job. The more time you devote to your job search, the greater the likelihood you will get the results you want.

You will be most effective if you establish a routine and stick to a schedule—one that coincides with the schedule of the people you will be contacting. This can be challenging and takes tremendous discipline. Consider it your training for the real job you soon will have.

Make a commitment to set an alarm so you can wake up early each day. Decide ahead of time how much time you will devote to your job search activities and include the number of calls you will make daily to keep your momentum going. In addition, you will benefit by establishing a network of people you can count on to support you during this time and, if possible, meet with on a regular basis.

GET UP AND GET DRESSED

When I began my career in sales I worked out of my home. It didn't take me long to figure out that I got more done when I got up and got dressed each day. Calling clients while wearing my robe and slippers didn't work. If I didn't take myself and my job seriously, how could I expect anyone else to take me seriously? Whether I was going to meet with someone in person or not, I got up each day and got ready as if I were.

It made a huge difference in the way I felt and in the way I came across to others, whether over the phone or by other correspondence.

Get up and get dressed, but not in your most comfortable sweats or jeans; put on something you'd wear to work. Try wearing the suit you plan to wear to an interview. If you only put it on when you have an interview, you may feel awkward wearing it for the interview. You might be surprised at how good dressing up makes you feel—and how much more productive you are when you do.

TURN IT OFF

When you are ready to begin your day, start by turning off the television. If you want background noise, turn on the radio or listen to soft background music. Television is distracting and you need to be focused.

Stay caught up on current events, but don't dwell on them. Listening to the same news stories over and over can be depressing. You are better off filling your mind with news about industry trends and other information related to your job search.

Avoid a lot of background noise when you are making phone calls or receiving calls, as it will be heard by the person on the other end of the line. You need to come across as favorably as possible, so eliminate anything that is a possible detriment.

If you have more than one phone, turn off those you are not using. Not only will this cut down on interruptions, but it will also prevent a phone from ringing when you are in the midst of talking with a potential employer.

Turn off call waiting. If you are unable to do this and a call comes in during a job-related conversation, do not answer it. Ignore it. Whenever you are having a job search- related conversation, your priority and attention should be on that call.

Turn off instant messaging. It is fine to check your e-mail, but don't carry on a conversation with your friends all day long. Use the Internet for your job search, not your social life. It's simply too easy to lose track of and waste time on the Internet. Use the Internet wisely and in ways that will benefit you and your job search.

Turn off *anything* that has the potential to disrupt you and close your door for privacy.

EXPAND YOUR KNOWLEDGE

Be sure you devote some part of each day to gaining new knowledge. This can be accomplished by talking to people, and through reading and research. Keep up on industry trends, read trade publications, research companies, do research on the Internet, and spend time at the library. Do whatever you can to keep learning and expanding your knowledge in all areas.

Become crystal clear about what you want from and what you bring to an organization. Face your fears and work at overcoming them. Try something new; take up a hobby or volunteer in your community. The more interested you are in gaining knowledge, the more interesting you will be to others. Be inquisitive; learn from others. Every person you talk with is another person you can learn from. Every company you learn about expands your understanding of the business world.

It is important to evaluate who you are and who you need to become to fit the role you are taking on and to fit into your desired business environment. Rather than trying to make this transition all by yourself, it will be much easier if you find someone to help you.

A frequent comment I heard from the executives I interviewed for this book was that young people need a mentor. It will benefit you if you can find someone who is willing to take you under his or her wing and not only provide advice but spend time helping you grow. A mentor may be a family member or friend or even someone you currently don't know. He or she could be someone in your chosen industry or a friend of a friend. Many companies have implemented mentoring programs, but until you have a job, you are on your own to find a mentor.

USE YOUR NETWORK OF PEOPLE

As you begin talking with people about your chosen profession, you will acquire valuable information as well as additional contacts. Each contact will lead to another contact, so don't hesitate to ask for names and phone numbers. It's always easier calling someone when you have a friend in common than calling someone when you don't have anything or anyone in common. Learning more about the career you are interested in is all about networking with others. It's probably how you've met many of your friends. Someone introduced you to someone else; that's what networking is all about.

My oldest daughter, Stephanie, was nearing the end of her high school years and becoming serious about her search for the right college. It wasn't until she began talking with others that she got some of her most valuable information. She would hear about a school and express interest in learning more about it and, sure enough, someone knew someone who went there. Happily, they would provide her with the name, telephone number, and e-mail address of that person. She was able to get all of her questions answered about that school once she connected with someone who went there.

You may have heard the adage, "It's not what you know, it's who you know." In other words, talking with and knowing the right people is important. Don't let the word "networking" worry you. Networking is just a fancy word for talking with people, forming relationships, asking the right questions, and getting the information you need. You talk to people every day. Perhaps you already are net-working, but if you aren't, you could be overlooking the possibilities that can evolve from asking the right questions of casual and not-so-casual acquaintances.

To successfully network, you must be willing to talk with people outside of your immediate circle of friends and family. This is the only way to effectively network and connect with the right people. For example, assume you are interested in advertising. You can't think of anyone you know who is in the field but you think your friend's brother works in advertising. Are you willing to call this friend and ask for his or her brother's telephone number?

In addition to friends, you can network with teachers; members of your church, synagogue, or mosque; neighbors; relatives; and people who belong to a variety of organizations. Most people enjoy helping others, but no one can help you if you don't ask. Start connecting and networking with others. It is the single most effective way to get the word out about your need for employment and to make new contacts.

IMPROVE YOUR "PACKAGE"

If you had two wrapped gifts placed in front of you and you were only able to open one of them, how would you decide which one to unwrap? Very likely the packaging would influence you. If one of the gifts was beautifully and professionally wrapped, and the other was haphazardly wrapped with wrinkled, recycled paper, which one would you choose as the gift you wanted to open and why?

Think of yourself as a gift to any company lucky enough to employ you. There are many gifts for employers to choose from. How can you best convince a prospective employer that you are the best gift for the organization or company?

A resume is the first thing a prospective employer sees, the first aspect of your package. Your resume provides a glimpse of who you are: your education, work history, and interests. Your resume is the first impression a prospective employer has of you. The objective of your resume is to present yourself well enough to be granted an interview. Make sure your resume represents you favorably. If it doesn't, you may never get the opportunity for an interview.

Once you are granted an interview, you can assume that your credentials were sufficient to get to this step. Now think about the person who is interviewing a number of candidates; this person wants to meet you to learn more about you—to see the rest of the package. If the candidates possess similar skills and background, how do you think an employer will go about choosing one over another?

Pay close attention to your overall presentation; your clothing, grooming, and body language. It is your overall presentation that will set you apart either positively or negatively from others.

Assuming your image is on par, are you an effective communicator? How you sound in person, on the phone, in e-mail, and on your answering machine is a part of your professional package.

If someone calls to set up an interview, and your answering machine plays a rap song or conveys off-color humor, what message will that send to a prospective employer?

If you plan on giving out your e-mail address and communicating on the Internet, evaluate your e-mail address. Asking a potential employer to contact you at Partygirl.com or Egomaniac.net may send the wrong message, especially during this critical time of initial assessment. Take a look at the many ways you communicate and see to it that all of your communication tools represent you positively and professionally.

PATIENCE IS A VIRTUE

As I conducted my research to determine some of the biggest challenges companies face with young, first-time professionals, patience was a common theme. "These kids come out of school expecting a lot," says Richard Lerner, CEO of RLM Public Relations in New York City, "and they don't always realize how much is ahead of them. They are motivated to get raises and expect to get them—fast."

You may be used to things happening fast, but in the business world, patience is a virtue. As you search for a job, be patient and wait for the right job before you accept a position. Don't become discouraged if your job search takes longer than expected, and try not to appear too eager for a position as though you are desperate for work. Although weeks can seem like months, the time you spend looking for a job is relatively brief compared to the number of years you will be working.

The attitude you adopt now will carry over into your career. You will have ups and downs in both your job search and your career. There will be good days and bad days, stressful days and easy days. Try to be realistic about what lies ahead for you. You may not find exactly what you want in your first job, but an offer that will give you the experience you need or provide opportunities for advancement may be worth taking. Be patient; keep your mind open and enjoy the journey.

SUMMARY

Remember

- ✔ Treat finding a job as a job. Set up a special workstation for your job search, and follow a schedule to ensure you spend some time each day pursuing new contacts and advancing your job possibilities.

- ✔ Maximize your network. Connect with as many people as possible. Ask everyone you know for contacts to help expand your network.

- ✔ Don't sit back hoping for something to come through; make something happen. Take control of your job search.

- ✔ Get up and get dressed. You will feel better when you stick to a work schedule. Getting dressed each day will help you get in the right frame of mind.

✔ Turn it off: Get rid of all distractions by turning off everything that could possibly distract you.

✔ Be patient. Don't expect things to happen overnight. You will find a job, but it may take some time. Remember that all good things are worth waiting for.

Chapter 5

Finding the Job You Want

FINDING A JOB TAKES TIME

Kavita Gosyne writes a column for graduates that appears weekly in the *Metro Toronto* newspaper. A recent grad herself, she realizes how naïve she was when she began looking for work soon after she graduated from college in 2004: "I thought I would graduate, send my resume to all the different places I wanted to work, and be hired within a month or two. I thought I just needed my degree in hand like it was my free parking pass." Looking back, she wishes someone had prepared her because finding a job was harder than she ever imagined. She assumed her degree would open doors, but it did not. "Graduating is just step one," she said. "Most grads are clueless about the amount of time it takes to find a good job. I don't think grads can understand the harsh reality until it hits them."

After months of frustration, Kavita decided to e-mail the editor at the *Metro*, where she had previously interned, about her dilemma, mentioning she had enough information to write a column about it. A month later she had a weekly column. Challenges are not always without payoffs—the column Kavita writes would never have come to be if not for her difficult experience in finding a job. Among the many lessons learned, Kavita realized she had more to offer than she thought and that she could beat the odds by being willing to work her way up. "Sometimes you have to go after what you want and make your own opportunities," Kavita advises.

CREATE A PLAN

Finding a job is not a quick or easy process. As you've already discovered in the previous chapters, you've got some work to do before you begin looking for work. Getting organized and in the right frame of mind is important, as is identifying what you want and what you have to offer. You need a carefully prepared resume and practice interviewing before you meet with potential employers. When you've got everything in place and are ready to get serious about finding a job, you need a plan of action. A well thought-out job-hunting strategy lets you know what you need to do and how to utilize your time wisely.

Start by determining a realistic time frame for finding a job. Consider the job market, the industry you want to work in, and your available time commitment in your job search. If you haven't yet got a resume or done any informational interviewing, you need to allow time to get yourself ready. If you are all set and ready to devote ample time to finding a job, you are likely to find one much sooner. Create your plan of action. How will you go about finding the job you want? How much time will you devote to your efforts each day? How many new contacts will you make? Which resources will you utilize? Create a daily, weekly, and monthly schedule to follow. Set target contact numbers and goals you want to accomplish.

Creating a plan of action is the easy part. Executing your plan can be much more difficult. No one is going watch over you, checking to make sure you do as you say or telling you what to do. This is *your* job search. It's up to you to take the first step and every step thereafter. You need to rely on *you* to keep your momentum going, but you don't have to do it all alone. If you want guidance, it's up to you to seek it out and get the help you need.

UTILIZE YOUR RESOURCES

When it comes to finding a job, there are scores of resources available. An abundance of information and advice is available to you through talking with people, reading books, and searching the Internet. You will find jobs listed online, on company Web sites, in the newspaper, through word of mouth, and more.

There are always jobs available, but you'll need to work at finding the one for you. Be resourceful and don't rely on any one method to find a job. Utilize as many methods as you can to learn and to connect with opportunities. The following are some of the best resources to utilize in your job search:

People

When you are looking for a job, your focus is on what you need and want. To be more effective, you must also focus on the needs of others—in particular, the people you are hoping will hire you. According to Peter Vogt, a Minneapolis career counselor and author of *Career Wisdom for College Students*, hiring a full-time employee carries a great deal of risk and expense. Companies spend large amounts of time and money in recruiting and advertising, interviewing and evaluating candidates, and putting together an offer. The person doing the hiring is under tremendous pressure to hire the right person. They are likely to go to any length possible to hire someone they already know and trust or who comes highly recommended by someone they know and trust.

Your best resource in finding a job is other people. Personal connections and referrals remain one of the most effective ways to find a job. Talking with others will help you learn more about your areas of interest, explore jobs and fields you may not be aware of, and discover unpublished opportunities.

It is up to you to reach out to others; don't expect others to get in touch with you. No one will know what you need unless you tell them. Ask others for advice, ask for information, and ask for the help you need. The more people you meet and chat with, the better. More jobs are found through word of mouth than any other resource.

Internships

There are many benefits of an internship. In addition to the experience, knowledge, and personal connections you will gain, you might just end up with a job offer. According to the National Association of Colleges and Employers' (NACE) *2004 Experiential Education Survey*, new college graduates who have participated in an internship or cooperative education assignment give themselves a "leg up" in the job market. Employers responding to NACE's survey reported that, on average, they extend offers for full-time employment to nearly 58 percent of the students who served internships with their organizations, and to more than 60 percent of those who have taken part in co-op assignments with them.

An internship provides you with many of the essentials for finding a job and getting hired. You already have connections with others in the organization, you're already somewhat trained, and they have a record of your job performance. Assuming you were a model employee, and the company was hiring, why wouldn't they consider you? You've already got your foot in the door—you're an insider now. You're less risky than someone from the outside. You may get a job offer whether you express interest in employment opportunities or not, but if you are interested in working for a company you interned with, let it be known.

Career centers

A valuable resource, yet often underused, is your school or college career center. If you haven't already, visit the career/counseling placement office at your school. Find out what services are available—most of which are free. Some schools offer on-site job interviews with prospective employers. Others hold informational workshops, or provide individual counseling, coaching, and mentoring. Many provide assessments to help you determine your interests and career direction. The majority of career centers offer a variety of other services including job postings, resume help, interview prep, and more.

Nothing will prepare you better for an interview than the experience itself. If your center provides the opportunity to conduct a mock interview, utilize that service. If you can get your interview on videotape, jump at the chance and review it repeatedly. While you may not enjoy watching yourself initially, you will adjust and benefit greatly. It is the only way to see yourself as you really are and to determine your strengths and areas that need work.

Company Web sites

Many companies post job openings on their corporate Web sites and this can be a great way for you to target companies you are interested in working for. Responses from over 400 job seekers suggest that corporate employment Web sites are perceived to be the most useful and confidential job search tool available through the Internet. The JOBcentral 2005 Job Seeker Survey, conducted by Dr. Rich Cober and Dr. Doug Brown of Booz Allen Hamilton, asked job seekers to differentiate between four online recruiting sources: online job boards, niche employment Web sites, professional association Web sites, and corporate employment Web sites.

Job seekers perceived company Web sites as the best place for finding jobs on the Internet as well as the online source providing them with the best chance of actually getting an interview and being offered a job. Be sure to visit the Web sites of the companies in which you are interested.

Direct contact

If you've got your eye on working for a particular company, one of the best ways to get your foot in the door is by making direct contact with someone in the organization. Even when there isn't an advertised position, it doesn't mean there is no opportunity for you. In fact, many positions are never advertised.

You can call and ask to speak to someone or send a letter and your resume by mail, and then follow up. When used in conjunction with other job search tactics, directly contacting companies can prove very valuable. It may not always lead to an immediate job offer, but if you are truly interested and stay connected, it could lead to an offer in the future.

Career and job fairs

Job fairs can be useful in many ways. They can save you time because you will be able to connect with a number of companies at once. You will meet many different people, learn about companies and positions you may not otherwise investigate, and you will gain practice meeting with and talking to potential employers. In order to maximize your time at a job fair, research the companies attending in advance and determine those you want to target. Additional tips on getting the most out of a job fair can be found in Chapter 10.

The Internet

One of the most easily accessible tools to aid you in your job search is the Internet. There are thousands of Web sites related to career exploration. There are general career information sites, sites for grads, and industry-specific sites designed to:

- Help you assess and identify your goals, skills, and interests

- Learn about specific occupations

- Determine where to acquire the necessary education and training for an occupation

- Determine if licenses or certifications are necessary for certain occupations

- Create and design a resume and cover letter

- Put together a career portfolio

- Find job openings

- Negotiate a job offer

- And much more

Chris Russell, President of AllCountyJobs.com and author of the blog "Secrets of the Job Hunt," suggests using the Internet as one of many tools in your job seekers toolbox. You are wise to rely on the Internet for research, but it shouldn't be used as the only method for finding work. A good strategy includes both online and "offline" methods. Russell suggests visiting sites such as LinkedIn.com or Indeed.com to save time and help build your "virtual" network.

Employment agencies

Employment agencies can be a good resource to use, particularly because they may be privy to job openings not posted elsewhere. An employment agency works with both companies and job seekers to fill open positions. There are several different types of agencies; some provide temporary employment (which in some instances can lead to permanent employment), others place people only in full-time permanent positions.

Agencies will either charge you a fee for their services and job placement or charge the employer the fee. Some agencies offer additional services and will work with you in your development, helping you assess your skills, personality, and ability. Visit a few agencies to gain a better understanding of what each does and determine the one that fits you best.

Associations and other group affiliations

The more active you are the better. And the more time you spend focused on activities to help you find a job, the greater your results will be. Broaden your resources and personal connections by getting involved in professional and industry associations, networking with your alumni association, and attending job support groups and any other groups you'd like to be affiliated with.

Sitting at home alone or commiserating with your unemployed friends will do nothing to help you find a job or lift your spirits. Push yourself to get out and meet with a variety of people. Stay connected and involved with others, regardless of your employment status. It will be good for your attitude and your job search.

Want ads

If you are relying on job postings in the classified section of your local newspaper to find a job, you need to expand your efforts. Considering many jobs (some say *most* jobs) are never advertised, the want ads should be used only as one of many methods in your job search. Read the classified section of your Sunday paper, but don't rely on it.

Other

Don't limit your job hunting to the above resources. Jobs are found in any number of ways. Some people have managed to create the job they want. Others have placed ads in newspapers and campaigned on their own behalf for a specific position. If you have an idea and are entrepreneurial, you might bring an idea to someone or even consider starting your own business. The more creative and flexible you are in your approach to finding a job, the better.

There is no right or wrong way to find work, but there are proven tactics that increase your chances. If you find a job quickly, you are fortunate, but don't plan on landing the job of your dreams in your first or second attempt.

You might find it helpful to work part time or find temporary work to generate income and keep yourself motivated as you look for your ideal job. *Every* experience you have and *everyone* you meet has the potential to help you and lead you to the job you seek. Seek out as many experiences and people as you can.

FOLLOW UP AND FOLLOW THROUGH

As you learned in the previous chapter, finding a job is a job; you need to put in as many hours as you can. When job seekers were asked how many hours they devoted to their job search each day in a JobDig.com survey in 2006, 36 percent of the respondents said they spend an hour a day on job search activities. Devote more time to your search and you will be heads above your competition.

Utilize a variety of methods as you go about finding a job. It increases your contacts and your chances of finding something. It is up to you to go after what you want, to be persistent, and to follow up, whether it's to make sure your resume arrived somewhere or to request an interview.

Keep notes of all contacts you make and every conversation you have, and refer to them often. Use a computer program to keep your job search records and addresses. Your hard work will be in vain if you fail to follow through as promised or lose a valuable contact name and number. Keeping everything in one place and organized so that you can access it easily is of vital importance.

View your job search as an exciting adventure and approach it enthusiastically. You'll not only enjoy yourself more, you'll be more likely to find what you are looking for if you do.

SUMMARY

Remember

✔ Finding a job takes time. Set realistic goals and don't worry if you don't find a job right away.

✔ Create a plan and follow that plan. The more prepared you are, the more effective you will be.

✔ Visit your school or college career center and utilize the services they offer.

✔ Seek out and attend job fairs.

✔ Use a variety of methods in your job search, including those both online and "offline."

✔ Get involved. Participate in group activities, network with others, and benefit from the help and advice of others.

✔ Keep detailed records of your activities, contacts, and conversations.

✔ Stay the course. Never stop working at finding a job; it may take you longer than you'd like, but as long as you are committed, active, and creative, you will find a job.

Chapter 6

Putting Yourself on Paper

CREATING A RESUME

You may already have a resume. You may think you know what a resume should look like. Or maybe writing your resume is one of the many tasks still to be done. Whatever your thoughts, I cannot emphasize strongly enough the importance of your resume. To a prospective employer, you are your resume. It is your initial introduction to a company and their first impression of you. Considering most employers spend only seconds looking at each resume, if yours is poorly written or produced it will end up in a file or pile somewhere–or worse yet, in the trash. Make sure your resume represents you in the best possible manner.

A resume should include your:

- Overall objective, which can be a statement summarizing your skills and talents, or about the position you are seeking

- Qualifications

- Education

- Skills

- Academic accomplishments

- Personal accomplishments

- Work experience (including your responsibilities and achievements)

- Employment history

- Contact information

Your resume needs to represent the best of who you are and, if prepared properly, it will secure interviews for you. Do all you can to make it easy for prospective employers to connect with you (especially during business hours), by providing them with as much information as possible. It is important to include your name, address, telephone number, and e-mail address so that, if interested, someone will know how to get in touch with you. A resume is not something that should be completed too quickly or without outside help. Utilize the services and information available to you. There are wonderful books written about resume writing, a number of Internet sites with valuable information, and resume services that will, for a fee, help you put together your resume. Take time to do some research before you begin to create your resume. The time and money you spend up front will be most worthwhile.

WHAT ARE YOU LOOKING FOR?

Imagine that you have decided to hire someone to help you with your job search. You want to make your decision carefully because this person will be instrumental in helping you identify what you want to do, assist you in developing your resume, help you connect with companies, and much more. You place an ad and receive a number of letters and resumes as a result. Because the response to your ad is so great, you need to find an efficient way to determine which responses are worth pursuing

As you glance through the pile of resumes, you notice that most are on plain white or off-white paper, but a few are on different shades—one is bright orange. Most are written in 10- to 12-point type and use standard fonts such as Helvetica, Times Roman, and Palatino. One of the resumes features a variety of font sizes and styles that make it stand out.

The majority of the resumes are one page, a few are two pages, and one is three pages long. A few are folded, some are stapled, and one is taped together. In addition to the resume, several applicants have included a letter, personally written to you, stating their interest in helping you find a job. You notice a misspelled word here and there and an incomplete sentence on one resume. One person has included a picture of himself with his resume, and another has listed personal data including age, height, and weight.

You want the person you hire to begin working for you as soon as possible, but the response has been so great that you realize you won't have time to meet with more than a handful of the people who responded to your ad.

How will you determine which people are worth meeting and what criteria will you use to help you decide? Remember, the only information you have is a resume from each person.

As you review the resumes, do you think you are likely to:

- Read every word on every resume to determine who is most qualified?

- Skim and scan the resumes quickly to determine which ones you want to pursue?

- Favor those with unusual fonts, style, or that are printed on colored paper?

- Disregard the one with the coffee stain on it?

- Read those with cover letters first?

- Pursue the one who sent the picture?

- Overlook typographical or grammatical errors?

Take time to think about your answers because it will help you as you make decisions about the resume you create. It can help to view your resume through the eyes of an employer. When you submit your resume to companies, it could be one of hundreds employers will see. You want to be certain your resume will sell you effectively and help you to be selected for an interview.

MOST COMMON MISTAKES

Susan Britton Whitcomb, author of *Resume Magic: Trade Secrets of a Professional Resume Writer* (QIST Works, 1998), defines a resume as an advertisement that should appeal to an employer's specific needs.

According to Whitcomb, some of employers' biggest pet peeves and the most common mistakes made on resumes include:

- Leaving out dates
- No chronological listing of work experience
- No listing of accomplishments
- Incomplete listing of accomplishments
- Fancy fonts
- Photos
- Typos
- Misspelled words
- Disorganized structure
- Too long

One way employers increase their efficiency is by eliminating the resumes with noticeable mistakes. When you send a resume you know is error free, you increase the likelihood it will be read.

PROOFREAD, PROOFREAD, THEN PROOFREAD AGAIN

Have you ever written a paper, looked it over, and submitted it, confident it was error free, and discovered afterward that it had a typo or mistake you overlooked? I know I have, and I am always stunned because once I see the error, I wonder how I ever overlooked it. Although many mistakes are minor, making it easy to see how they were overlooked, occasionally I will notice a mistake that is so obvious that it is hard to believe I didn't catch it myself.

Any document you work on for a period of time eventually becomes difficult to view objectively. Given that your resume is so crucial to your future, it can become even more difficult for you to be impartial. It is a good idea to have several people (trusted friends, your parents, a teacher, etc.) proofread your resume before submitting it to ensure it is error free. The more people you have look it over, the better your chances of catching any and all mistakes.

Prepare your resume in advance, before you need to send it out. When we don't take time to step away from a document, we lose our ability to be objective. The more you do this, the better. Each time you step away and come back to the document you are likely to see something you didn't see before. If you are in a hurry to get your resume done, you won't have the time you need to make sure it is complete.

Resumania is the term hiring expert Robert Half, founder of Accountemps, a staffing service, coined to describe the blunders that have appeared in resumes, job applications, and cover letters. Hiring managers who receive documents with mistakes, misused words, or inappropriate information may toss them or worse yet, put them in their own Resumania file. The following are a few examples of real resume blunders:

- Worked party-time as an office assistant

- Planned and held up meetings

- Thank you for beeting me for an interview

- Computer illiterate

- I am entirely through in my work; no detail gets by me

You want your resume to generate interest, not laughs. Take the time to make sure your resume is error free.

PRESENTATION IS EVERYTHING

It may seem that with the capabilities of the Internet, the preferred way to send a resume would be e-mail, but never assume it is. Send your resume in the format the employer prefers.

When you do send your resume electronically, include the position you are applying for and your name in the subject line of the e-mail.

Make sure you label your resume attachment with your name as well. Receiving hundreds of documents titled "resume" can he confusing to a prospective employer.

Hand delivering a resume assures you that it will arrive in perfect condition, but is not always feasible. Whether you mail your resume or personally deliver it, do what you can to make sure it looks good when it gets into the hands of the right person. Your resume will look best if you:

- **Keep it flat.** Folding a resume is not recommended, nor is stapling or taping sheets together. Purchase envelopes that are the same size as the paper you are using.

- **Keep it neutral.** Resumes on colored paper will stand out, but not in a positive way. Neutral colors (white, off-white, pale gray) are most commonly used for resumes and are preferred by employers. Print your resume on high quality, neutral-colored paper.

- **Keep it clean and error free.** Make sure there are no errors, marks, or stains on your resume.

- **Keep it simple.** Your resume should be easy to read and easy to scan. Leave enough white space and spacing so that the information isn't crammed together. Bulleted information is another way to make a resume easy to read.

- **Keep it brief.** Keep your resume to one page whenever possible. A brief resume is preferred, but the length of your resume should be determined by the necessary information that will best sell you to the employer. The main goal is to send the right message and convey your qualifications. One to two pages is standard for a typical resume.

- **Keep it standard.** Do what you can to make your resume distinctive, but don't make it too unusual or you may not be taken seriously. Including a picture or personal information is not necessary and not recommended.

- **Keep it truthful.** You may be tempted to lie in order to make yourself appear more qualified, but resist the temptation. An employer is likely to verify some or all of the information on your resume. Not only will you lose the trust of your employer if you are found out, you could lose your job.

COVER YOUR BASES WITH A COVER LETTER

One way to add a personal touch is by including a cover letter with your resume. This letter differs from a resume as it is written to the person doing the hiring and will most likely be read before he or she takes a look at your resume. Although some people feel a cover letter is optional, many experts advise applicants never to submit a resume without one. A survey conducted by the Society for Human Resource Management reported that 67 percent of resumes received today by human resources (HR) departments are accompanied by a cover letter.

You want to do everything you can to make sure your resume is reviewed and that it successfully communicates who you are; a cover letter increases your chances of getting noticed. There are no guarantees someone will read your letter, but there are things you can do to increase the likelihood that it will be read.

As you create your resume and cover letter, focus on the employer and his or her needs, interests, and priorities rather than your own. What do you think an employer wants to hear? What will motivate someone to call you in for an interview?

Because this document is a letter, it is important to treat it like any other letter you would write. A cover letter can be more personal than a resume, but don't stray too far from a traditional business letter. Each letter should be crafted for its reader, so do some investigating before writing it. Address it to a specific person, sign it in ink, and always submit the original copy. In addition, as with the resume, you want to make sure your cover letter is brief and error free.

Dr. Randall S. Hansen, an employment consultant and coauthor of *Dynamic Cover Letters* (Ten Speed Press, 2001), reveals the three most common cover letter mistakes:

1. **Not addressing a letter to a named individual.** In most situations, job seekers who go the extra mile can find the name of the person they need to write to for a job interview. Avoid sexist salutations (i.e. Gentlemen, Dear Sir), and titles (Dear Human Resource manager). Taking the time to find the name of the individual is much more effective.

2. **Failing to be proactive by requesting an interview.** Job seekers need to take the initiative in cover letters and ask for the interview. You should only be writing the letter if you feel you are qualified for the position, so don't end the letter weakly by saying something like "I look forward to hearing from you." Instead, end the letter by stating, "I will call you the week of October 3 to set up an interview."

3. **Telling what the company can do for you rather than what you can do for the company.** Employers don't care that hiring you will fulfill one of your lifelong ambitions; instead, they want to know what you can do for them. Job seekers need to show potential employers that they can make an immediate impact on the job.

In Chapter 2, you had the chance to think about the types of words that best describe who you are. Because a cover letter and resume are your introduction, you want to use words that will hopefully move the reader to action—by asking you for an interview.

Avoid wishful thinking, such as "I hope you will find my resume impressive." Instead, make assertive, powerful statements such as "I am certain you will find my experience and skills to be an excellent match to the qualifications you seek for this position."

Don't be afraid to say, "I am an excellent candidate for this position and I look forward to meeting with you." You must sell yourself and your strengths, convincing the employer you are worth meeting.

Always end your letter by thanking the person for their time and stating your next move as specifically as you can by saying, "I will call you on (name the date)," "I will contact you next week," or "You can expect to hear from me by (name the date)." This shows that you are a person who will take charge and take the lead. If you say you will call on a certain day, be sure to do as you say. Nothing will discredit you faster than failing to follow through on your promises.

REFERENCES

Once a company is interested in you, you're likely to be asked to provide references. Usually, providing two or three references is sufficient. Always seek permission before using someone as a reference. You wouldn't want anyone to be shocked to receive a call and become tongue-tied when answering questions about you.

Select your references carefully and choose people from different areas of your life—family members are not recommended. Try to include someone you have worked for or with, someone who knows you personally, and someone who knows you academically. You may want to ask a few people to write reference letters or letters of recommendation so that you can give them to a hiring manager, if requested.

THE TELEPHONE IS A USEFUL TOOL

Once you've worked hard to create the perfect resume and have submitted it to a number of companies, you hope it will do its job and help you obtain interviews. But don't sit back and wait for employers to contact you, because if you do, the phone may never ring.

If you want to be noticed, do something to stand out. Make yourself visible by calling and letting people know who you are. You can call to verify that your resume arrived safely, to inquire about the status of the position, or to reaffirm your interest in the position. It is best to talk directly with the decision maker when possible, but many times you will not get past an assistant. This is fine and the assistant may be able to provide you with valuable information about the company, the job that you applied for, and the pace of the interviewing process.

While you don't want to become a pest, you do need to take control of as much of the job-hunting process as you can. If you sense your calls are unwelcome, back off, but ask questions to help you determine how to proceed. Keep in mind the following tips when you are faced with making a difficult call:

- Have a purpose for your call

- Begin with an appropriate salutation such as "good morning," "good afternoon," or "hello"

- Introduce yourself by name

- State the purpose of your call

- Ask for someone by name when possible

- Speak in an enthusiastic and upbeat manner

- Ask for help. Say: "Are you able to suggest a next step for me?" or "Do you have any suggestions as to how I might schedule an appointment for an interview?"

- Always thank someone for speaking with you or helping you

- Leave a message with your name and number when possible

- Develop an outline or script to follow prior to making calls and consider practicing what you want to say to help you become more comfortable

SUMMARY:

Remember:

- ✔ Take your time when preparing your resume to ensure it does its job, which is to get you noticed and obtain interviews.

- ✔ Seek the advice of others when preparing your resume, and have several people proofread it before you submit a copy to anyone. Typos or mistakes will immediately disqualify you as a candidate for most positions.

- ✔ Keep your resume brief and reader-friendly. Limit your resume to one page whenever possible and use bullets, lists, and an easy-to-read font, point size, style, and format.

✔ Use neutral-colored paper and make sure your resume is free of stains and marks.

✔ Write a cover letter addressed directly to the hiring person and include it with your resume. This will enable you to personalize yourself and your resume, and will give you an advantage over those who omit this step.

✔ Speak affirmatively. Never use words such as "hope" or "wish." Assert yourself and let a potential employer know that you know you can do the job. Rather than asking for an interview, request one.

✔ Follow up with a telephone call. Make a call to ensure your resume arrived, to check the status of the position, or to ask for an interview. Befriend assistants or anyone you talk with and don't be afraid to ask for help. The telephone can be your best tool if you use it wisely.

✔ Make it easy for an employer to reach you, especially during business hours. Include telephone numbers and an e-mail address in all of your communications. If it becomes too challenging for an interested employer to reach you, he or she will give up.

Chapter 7

Prepare for Interview Success

PREPARING FOR THE INTERVIEW

You've identified the type of job you are looking for. You have a sense of who you are, what you want, and what you have to offer. You've been talking with people, have conducted informational interviews, and may have had an internship. You've invested time creating the perfect resume. So, by the time you receive a call to set up an interview, your hard work has paid off.

A request for an interview indicates you have passed the criteria necessary to warrant a face-to-face meeting and someone is interested in learning more about you. You can assume your resume has represented you sufficiently to proceed to the next level of your job search. Congratulations! You've worked hard to get to this point, but you've still got a lot of work to do.

Some people fail to properly plan for an interview. They inaccurately assume that all they need to do to receive a job offer is validate their credentials and impress the interviewer. It isn't that simple. Properly planning for an interview involves much more.

Every interview will be different. Each interviewer you meet has his or her own style of interviewing. You may find you hit it off and relate better with some interviewers than others. Some interviewers will purposely create a stressful interview environment to see firsthand how you handle yourself under duress. Some interviews will be complex, others quite simple. Some interviews will be brief; others will last longer. It all depends on the nature of the position and the interview techniques the interviewer or company uses.

No matter how prepared you think you are, you can never be certain about what type of interview you will have or what questions will be asked. Whether the interview you have scheduled is in person, on the phone, in a restaurant, or at a job fair, the more prepared you are, the better off you are.

DO YOUR HOMEWORK

As one employer stated, "I was always taught never to go into an interview without knowing something about the company. Today, four out of five applicants who are asked, 'What do you know about our company?' expect me to tell them rather than research on their own. And it is so easy to do these days, with most companies having a Web site or at least being mentioned on the Web somewhere! It seems to me to be just common courtesy and common sense to know something about the company you want to work at."

This may sound like common sense, but it isn't. One person who does a lot of interviewing told me he always starts out an interview by asking the candidate to tell him about his or her resume. Surprisingly, not everyone is able to respond.

If you can't talk about your background as it is reflected on your resume, it is a red flag to a potential employer. After all, it's *your* resume; know what's on it and make sure you can talk about the chronological sequence of events.

Spend time researching the company with whom you are interviewing, the industry, and the competition, so that you come to an interview ready to ask intelligent and specific questions. You can find information through company literature, online searches, the public library, and a variety of reference materials including articles from magazines, newspapers, and trade journals. Become familiar with the company's Web site, its mission statement, and annual reports.

In your search, seek to gain an understanding of the challenges this company has faced and the direction in which it is headed. The more you know about a company and, in particular, the position you are interviewing for, the better able you will be to communicate what you bring to that organization.

One of the best resources for obtaining information is by talking with employees who are already working there. Consider visiting the company a few days prior to your scheduled interview. You can learn a lot simply by observing.

Introduce yourself to the receptionist. This person might be able to provide you with additional information or connect you with someone who can. Be respectful of time and keep your conversations brief and thank anyone who takes time to help you.

Find out all you can about the position you are applying for and what qualities the ideal candidate will possess. When you understand what an employer is seeking, you can address his or her concerns and emphasize the qualities you possess that are important to the position.

ASKING AND RESPONDING TO QUESTIONS

There are many unknowns in an interview, but you can be certain you will be asked to provide information about yourself. Many interviewers begin an interview by saying, "Tell me a little about yourself." Don't wait until you are in an interview to decide what your response will be. Anticipate some of the questions you are most likely to be asked, such as: "What are your greatest strengths or outstanding qualities?" "How do you react under pressure?" "Why should I hire you?" "Why do you want to work here?" "What are your long-term career goals?" and "What are your weaknesses?"

Prepare short and concise answers to these and other similar questions you might be asked, without creating a memorized script. You want to respond as naturally and conversationally as possible, emphasizing what you *can* do and what you offer. Focus on what you've learned and how you've overcome challenges—even when talking about a weakness. For example, if a weakness of yours is that you tend to overcommit, you might explain that you've realized that overcommitting leads to stress and that you are better off saying no than agreeing to do something and failing to follow through. In this type of response you've demonstrated you acknowledge a weakness, learned from it, and have worked through it to your advantage.

In addition, think about how you will respond to unanticipated questions when they arise. You may be asked to recall a challenging or difficult situation and how you triumphed over it. You might be presented with a hypothetical problem and then asked to explain how you would go about solving that problem. You could be asked to talk about an achievement you are most proud of or to recall a time you failed and the reasons why. Be prepared to answer any question you are asked intelligently, thoughtfully, and *specifically*. Think about and have in mind specific examples and stories you can use in your responses. Expect the unexpected; decide ahead of time how you will respond to a question when you're not sure how to respond. Whatever you do, speak the truth; never lie or exaggerate in an interview. Once you are employed, if your employer discovers you were not truthful you could lose your job.

Diane has worked in human resources for over 20 years and has interviewed hundreds of job candidates. She says that the biggest mistake people make when interviewing is that they are too general when answering questions. She says she can tell when someone has done their homework; it is evident in the way that person responds to questions. Diane told me about the time she was interviewing someone for a sales position. When asked why he wanted to be in sales, he replied, "Because I heard you can make a lot of money in sales." He didn't get the job.

Employers want to hire people who will contribute something to the organization. You need to convince an employer that you understand what he or she needs and that you can meet those needs. You must be able to communicate what you bring to the position and the organization.

You must also be prepared by having a few questions of your own to ask. This should come from your natural curiosity and your desire to find the best position for you. Prepare unique and intelligent questions specifically geared to the particular position, company, and industry you are interviewing with.

Don't ask questions that you can easily find the answers to by reading a company brochure or by visiting its Web site. Ask questions you really want to know answers to: Are you interested in understanding the day-to-day functions of the job? Do you want to know what skills are needed to succeed in the job? Are you curious about knowing how your performance will be evaluated, why the position is open, or what the work environment is like? If so, ask.

Martin Yate, author of the *Knock 'Em Dead* book series, says, "People respect what you inspect, not what you expect." It is fine to inquire about the interviewer—what he or she likes about the company and how long he or she has worked there. In addition to providing you with firsthand information it will help you build rapport with the person interviewing you.

MAXIMIZE EVERY MINUTE

In a survey developed by Accountemps, a temporary staffing service, executives of the nation's 1,000 largest companies were asked this question: How many minutes into an interview do you know whether or not a candidate is a fit for the job?

The mean response was 16 minutes. "Applicants must be able to present a summary of their qualifications in a concise, enthusiastic, and poised manner, or they may lose their relatively short window of opportunity," says Max Messmer, chairman of Accountemps. "During the initial minutes of an interview, managers will be assessing whether candidates should move to the next step in their hiring processes, which may include additional interviews and skills tests as well as having references verified."

When you meet a prospective employer for the first time, make it your goal to appear in a way that reinforces the information on your resume and surpasses that person's expectations. Preparation is the key.

Being prepared for an interview involves more than skillfully responding to the questions you are asked. You must conduct yourself in a manner that tells others you are as capable as you say you are. Your personal presentation is as important, if not more important, as your qualifications and responses in an interview.

Steven Rothberg, president and founder of online career site CollegeRecruiter.com, told me about the young woman who came to an interview in a leather jacket and skirt. She was very qualified and presented herself well, but her choice of clothing left him feeling uneasy. The fact that she wasn't wearing more appropriate interview attire overshadowed her otherwise impressive presentation. Fortunately for her, he decided to meet with her one more time even though he was unsure. She came to the second interview dressed more appropriately for work and he offered her the job, which, upon looking back, he says, was the right decision.

You may not be so lucky. Not everyone will give you the benefit of the doubt or a second chance. Initial impressions are lasting; in an interview, you may never get a second chance if you don't make the right impression the first time.

HOW TO IMPRESS WHEN YOU'RE UNDER DURESS

Most people experience some nervousness before an interview. Don't let your apprehension get the best of you. Even seasoned performers experience some nervousness before a performance, which can actually help to stimulate a great performance. As one actress said, "Either I suffer, or my work does."

Hall of Fame basketball player Bill Russell became sick before every game he played. His teammates claimed that the sicker he got, the better he played. You don't need to become ill before an interview to do well; the key is to use your nervousness to your advantage. Turn it into positive energy and excitement.

If possible, travel to the location of the interview the day before so you can gauge the time it will take to get there and to ensure you won't get lost. Your preparation will reduce some of your stress and improve your chances for a successful interview.

Anticipate some nervousness, but don't let it consume you. If you are prepared, you really don't have anything to be nervous about. One of the best methods of preparation is by conducting a mock interview. Whether it's done through your college career center, a trusted individual, or a trained professional, the more you practice and get feedback, the better you will be. The interview should be videotaped, if possible, for nothing is as telling as seeing yourself on video. Although it can be uncomfortable to do and to watch, the information and practice you gain make it worthwhile.

Whatever you do, *practice.* Practice your entrance, your hand-shake, asking questions, and responding to questions. The more you practice, the better you will feel going into an interview. The better you feel, the more confidence you will have, and the more confident you are, the more likely you are to do well in an interview.

BE YOURSELF

Chas, a partner in an accounting firm, says that when he is interviewing job candidates, he looks for people who are comfortable with themselves. Some people would come to life when asked about a personal interest or hobby, and he would get a better sense of that person. Yet, some people never come to life at all. They go through the interview process robotically.

Most people feel a little nervous during an interview, but if you are so uptight that the interviewer can't get a sense of who you are, it could get in your way. Be personable; let others get to know who you are.

This entire chapter is about preparing for the interview. The thought of interviewing is stressful for most people. You know you are being evaluated and that you are in a competition you are not sure you can win. When you've done all you can to prepare for interview success, the only thing you can be sure you'll do better than anyone else is to be you. Let your personality shine through.

SUMMARY:

Remember:

✔ Do your homework. Gather as much information as you can about the industry, the company, and its competition. The more information you have, the better off you will be.

✔ Know what's on your resume. Be prepared to talk about your background and experience, including what's on your resume.

✔ Prepare responses to questions you are likely to be asked and practice what you will say when asked to talk about yourself.

✔ Put on the suit and shoes you will wear prior to the interview and get comfortable sitting, standing, and walking in this attire. Practice walking into an interview and shaking hands. The more comfortable you are, the better off you are.

✔ Do a trial run. Travel to the location of the interview a few days before the actual interview. Determine how much travel time you need and where to park. This will ease your stress the day of the interview.

✔ Be yourself. Although there are many things to think about in order to come off as well as you'd like, you don't want to come off robotically or artificially. Let your personality shine through; be your best, but be yourself.

✔ Expect some nervousness. Think of your nervousness as excitement and anticipation, then use it to your advantage.

Chapter 8

Dressing For Interview and Career Success

PROFESSIONAL APPEARANCE: A SENSITIVE SUBJECT

When I started my business, it was with the idea that I would help people improve their effectiveness in their jobs by becoming more professional in their appearance, behavior, and attitude. After being certified by the Professional Image Institute in Atlanta, I was ready to call on companies. I'll never forget the comment from the tenant who worked down the hall from my office. "You're into image consulting, aren't you?" he asked. I nodded and smiled as he continued, "So what exactly do you *do*—remind men to keep their zippers up and things like that?" He chuckled as he spoke, but I didn't see the humor. I wondered what I had gotten myself into and worried that others, too, would make light of what I do.

At first, it took a lot of courage for me to call companies and ask for an appointment, but once I had the opportunity to sit down and talk with a manager, human resources director, or president of a company, I discovered many of them shared similar concerns about the image and behavior of their employees.

Everyone I spoke with had concerns about certain employees who unknowingly sabotaged their careers because they didn't understand the relationship between personal appearance and opportunities for advancement. However, addressing such sensitive and personal issues with an employee was something that many managers chose to avoid because it was such a difficult task. No one wants to be the one to tell someone that he or she has poor hygiene, bad breath, or outdated clothing. It's not easy to inform someone you care about that he or she needs to dress differently or get a new hairstyle.

Rarely is the topic of personal appearance discussed in employee reviews, yet I've heard countless stories from individuals who attribute a promotion or pay raise to the fact that they dressed better than they needed to and "looked" as though they were ready for advancement. I've also heard from managers who didn't promote someone because the person didn't look ready to take on more responsibility. Unless an image problem is offensive enough to warrant a conversation, it is seldom mentioned, leaving many people clueless as to why they are being overlooked and not progressing in their careers.

Not only are there legal concerns about possible discrimination when approaching someone on such a personal level, but also the subject is so sensitive that it's easier to avoid it or delegate it to someone else. I've been hired to talk about the subject that nobody else wants to discuss. There have been times when I've addressed a group of 30 people because one or two people in that group needed to hear the message, but the company felt everyone could benefit as well.

You can gain something from this chapter whether you place importance on appearance or not. Fair or not, the way you look is important and ultimately, may influence your future more than you realize.

DO YOU NEED TO IMPROVE YOUR IMAGE?

What you wear and the way you look makes a statement about who you are and how you feel about yourself. Most people agree that judging others on appearances alone is unfair. Some people simply have an advantage when it comes to appearance. But most people, even those who are conventionally good looking, if asked, would say they'd like to change something about their appearance. One person might want to be taller; another longs to be shorter. One person feels too thin; the other feels too fat. Some people are blessed with great looks, which can be both an advantage and a disadvantage. If you are too good looking, people may resent you or view you as superficial. On the other hand, some people make negative snap judgments about those who are not conventionally attractive.

When it comes to achieving success, what you do with what you have and how you present yourself is much more important than natural beauty. Many people excel in spite of their perceived shortcomings. Being comfortable with yourself is the key. When you are at ease with who you are, you will radiate an inner and outer attractiveness. Take a moment to answer yes or no to the following questions:

- Does it take you more than a few minutes to decide what to wear each day?

- Do you frequently change outfits after getting dressed?

- Do you find shopping (when it comes to buying clothes) a chore?

- Do you often feel that you are either over- or under-dressed for an occasion?

- Do you often apologize for your appearance?

- Do people say that you look younger than you are?

- Do you wear unusual colors or styles?

- Do most people dress better than you?

- Do you try hard to look trendy?

- Do you wear rings or earrings on or in places other than your fingers and ears?

- Do you have visible tattoos?

- Do you think you look *different* from everyone else?

If you answered yes to any of the questions, you have identified some areas where you may be able to improve your image. If you didn't answer yes to any of the questions, you may have less work to do but will still benefit by increasing your knowledge about the importance of your appearance and how you can enhance your image.

YOUR IMAGE IS IMPORTANT

Many people don't want to believe that image matters. People don't like the thought of judging others on their looks, but the reality is that we all make decisions about people based on appearances. After all, initially it's the only information we have about someone.

Think about your favorite musicians. Many people have the ability to sing or play a musical instrument, but what is it that creates a superstar? It has a lot to do with image. Hundreds of thousands of dollars are spent creating and marketing just the right image for many superstars.

As a teen or young adult, you've probably felt at one time or another some pressure to fit in—especially in the clothing that you wear. You might pay more for a particular brand of jeans that everyone is wearing even though there are jeans mass marketed that cost significantly less. Simple T-shirts can be purchased for less than $10, but the same T-shirt with the logo of a popular store or brand of clothing will sell for two to three times that amount, and people willingly spend more in order to display the logo.

The clothing we wear does more than serve the function of covering our bodies or keeping us warm. Clothing and appearance often define our status and how we feel about our environment and ourselves. This has been going on for centuries in all cultures around the world.

Some people purposely draw attention by adorning themselves in metal and chains and dying their hair unusual colors. This is done with one purpose in mind: to make a statement. These people certainly fit in with others who dress as they do, but not with the mainstream, and this is done intentionally

Think about your group of friends. Do most of you tend to wear a similar style of clothing? Perhaps many of you wear your hair in a similar style. How do you feel around groups of people who dress differently from your group of friends? Do you view them as unusual?

The reality is that most of us feel more comfortable around people who look and act as we do. We tend to favor the expected over the unexpected, the usual over the unusual.

Imagine you are boarding a plane. You greet the flight attendant and look to the left into the cockpit. Two people are seated at the control panels. Both are dressed casually; one is wearing overalls and the other is in cut-off shorts and a Mickey Mouse T-shirt. One has sunglasses around his neck, the other a cap on backwards.

Assuming that these people are not passengers, who do you conclude is seated in the cockpit—the pilots or the mechanics? Most people would assume people dressed that way are the mechanics; but what if you discovered that these people are your pilots? Perhaps they had decided to dress casually on this day. Would you care?

I've found that most people say they would care and that it is important for a pilot to *look* like a pilot. But does it really matter what a pilot wears? Let's look at a few more situations, and you decide if the clothing worn makes a difference.

Does it matter:

- What is worn to a prom or a formal dance?

- What a bride and groom wear at their wedding?

- What you wear when you go swimming?

- What team members wear when playing a sport?

- What is worn to a costume party?

- What a priest, minister, or rabbi wears to conduct services?

- What a police officer wears when on duty?

- What an orchestra conductor wears when performing?

- What a nurse or doctor wears when seeing patients?

- What Olympic contestants wear when they compete?

You will probably agree that in all of the above circumstances the clothing worn *does* matter. Wearing the appropriate clothing to work can help you mentally prepare for the job. In addition, wearing the proper clothing can help you to fit in and feel a part of a team. Wearing what is expected enables us to identify people and their positions. Because human nature is somewhat predictable, we know that most people feel comfortable with others who look and act as they do.

What does your clothing reveal?

What are you wearing right now? It probably depends upon where you are as you are reading this, but if I could see you, what do you think your clothing would tell me (or others) about you?

Are you telling me (or others):

I care about my appearance *or*
I don't care about my appearance?

I dress for the occasion *or*
I wear what I want?

I spend a lot of money on my clothes *or*
I don't spend a lot of money on my clothes?

I got dressed in a hurry *or*
I took my time getting dressed?

I pay attention to detail *or*
I don't pay attention to detail?

I care what other people think of me *or*
I don't care what other people think of me?

How quickly do you think I would be able to determine these things about you? Do you realize it would only take me (or anyone else) a matter of seconds to determine how you feel about yourself and others, based solely on your image? It may not seem right, but we all make snap judgments about people based on their appearance. Considering the fact that your appearance communicates loudly about who you are, you should really think about what you wear every day.

YOUR CLOTHING COMMUNICATES

According to the results of a February 2005 survey by OfficeTeam, a staffing service specializing in highly skilled administrative professionals, 81 percent of employees polled said a person's work attire affects his or her professional image. Nearly half of the respondents said wardrobe significantly impacts how someone is perceived on the job.

The way you present yourself makes a statement about how you feel about yourself. Your clothing is the first thing people notice about you and communicates many things. What you wear will be noticed and influence others' opinions of you whether you intend it to or not.

Your clothing can communicate:

- Your sense of style

- Your degree of success

- Your social rank

- Your feelings about yourself

- Your feelings about your job

- Your feelings about the person or people you are with

- Your attitude

- Your level of sophistication

- Your financial status

- Your respect or lack of respect for others

Think about a day when you weren't feeling well. Perhaps it was a day when you wished you could stay home in bed but couldn't.

Would you put on a favorite outfit or opt for something that more closely matched your feelings? When we feel lousy, most of us prefer to look lousy too. In fact, on a lousy day we may actually look for something awful to wear rather than putting on something that we typically feel good in. Imagine putting on one of your favorite outfits, something you typically feel good in, on a day you were feeling lousy. Do you think it would affect the way you feel? Even if you don't feel well but you shower, fix your hair and dress up, you're likely to find that you feel better as a result.

Something happens when we go through the process of getting ready for work. Whether applying makeup, styling your hair, or putting on a uniform, each step helps you to physically and mentally prepare for your day. When you look as though you took the time to prepare for a meeting or your job, people notice. Through your appearance you are telling people you take yourself seriously and, as a result, you will find people view you more positively.

INFLUENCING POTENTIAL EMPLOYERS

The National Association of Colleges and Employers (NACE) Job Outlook 2006 Survey provided employers with a list of appearance-related attributes and asked them to indicate the degree of influence each would have on their opinion of a candidate's suitability for employment. Nearly three-quarters of respondents said a candidate's grooming would have a strong influence on their opinion of the candidate, and nearly half cited nontraditional interview attire as exerting a strong influence.

"A candidate's overall appearance is most likely to give a potential employer pause," says Marilyn Mackes, executive director of NACE. Grooming earned a 2.6 rating on a 3-point scale (where 1 = no influence, 2 = slight influence, and 3 = strong influence).

Employers also rated the following:

- Nontraditional interview attire (2.3)

- Handshake (2.1)

- Nontraditional hair color (2.0)

- Obvious tattoos (2.0)

- Body piercing (2.0)

- Unusual hairstyle (1.9)

- Earrings on male recruits (1.6)

- Beard (1.2)

- Mustache (1.1)

No matter how little importance you place on your appearance, when you are looking for a job, your appearance is important. It is the first thing noticed and it will be remembered. Don't worry about losing your individuality; you can be who you are and still present yourself professionally. Keep in mind that what you might feel is a distinctive trait (for example, the ring in your nose, unusual tattoo, or unique hair color) could be the one and only thing that gets in the way of a prospective employer viewing you as a viable candidate for a job.

An interviewer needs to narrow down the selection of candidates and therefore is *looking* for reasons to *eliminate* you as a prospect. Why take a chance on anything that might diminish your chances of having a successful interview?

WHAT TO WEAR TO AN INTERVIEW: IMPORTANT FACTORS TO CONSIDER

"What should I wear?" is an important question to ponder when preparing for an interview. Although most people have a suit reserved for interviewing, many are uncertain about wearing it when they discover the organization they are interviewing with is "casual." My advice is consistent: If you are interviewing for a professional position, you need to look professional. Although the person you are meeting with and others you see may be dressed casually, they can dress that way because they are already employed and a part of the organization, but you are not. You are an outsider competing against a number of other qualified and competitive candidates and must do everything you can to prove that you are a viable candidate to be considered.

When deciding what to wear to an interview, go for the expected over the unexpected, the usual over the unusual. Don't worry about being overdressed. If you want to work in a professional environment, dress professionally. A suit is considered traditional interview attire and is therefore the most expected attire, which makes it a wise choice.

Most people recognize the need to dress well for an interview. However, few people understand the importance of dressing well day after day, long after the interview is over. You will make many decisions that impact your career. One decision you will make every day is what you wear. This decision will affect the way you feel and will create a certain feeling among others. There are a number of factors to consider when deciding what to wear, so that you can present yourself in the best possible manner.

Your Employer

Your employer assumes you will present yourself at work in the same positive and professional manner in which you presented yourself when interviewing for the job. Be consistent in your appearance, positively representing your employer and company at all times. Managers don't want to be the fashion police; use good judgment in your clothing selection. If you have concerns or questions about what to wear, ask your supervisor for clarification.

The Climate

Although most offices are climate controlled, weather is an influencing factor when choosing what you wear. For example, in warmer weather you may want to eliminate layers of clothing in order to be comfortable, but removing too much clothing or revealing too much skin is not advised. One simple solution is to wear lightweight fabrics.

Your Personal Style

If you have unusual taste in clothing and dress much differently than others, your style has the potential to overshadow your ability.

Notice what others are wearing. Notice how others in your organization dress; pay particular attention to those in positions of authority for guidance on what to wear. There are ways to dress within the expected norm while maintaining your individuality, but it may take some time to develop your own personal style.

Your Customers

We all have expectations about those whose services we seek, and your clients and customers have expectations of you. When you meet these expectations you eliminate potential barriers. Dress in a manner that shows respect for yourself, your company, and your customers.

Your Industry

If you work for a high-tech or graphic design firm, the dress expectations will be different than if you work in an established, traditional industry such as accounting or banking. Each industry has its own image standards; know the standards of your industry and determine how to dress accordingly.

Your Position

Your position and the functions of your job will influence what you wear. If your job requires you to be physically active (bending, moving, etc.), you will need to dress accordingly.

DRESS FOR THE POSITION YOU WANT, NOT THE ONE YOU HAVE

Dressing better than expected lets others know you are serious about your career and can help you appear ready to move to the next level. Craig Kaminer, president of Influence, LLC, a strategic marketing, communications, and Internet development agency, recalls his first job as the director of public relations at the Jan Stuart Corporation, a manufacturer and marketer of upscale fragrance and skin care products. The office environment was very casual. A warehouse took up most of the space in the building; there were just 10 executive offices. Craig's office was located immediately next to the owner, Jan Stuart.

When he started the job, fresh out of college, Craig wanted to fit into the executive ranks of the company. He was told he could dress casually whenever he wanted, but he soon discovered that dressing casually was not in his best interest.

On the days he dressed casually, Craig noticed he was asked to do tasks outside of his job description. Jan would ask him to get him coffee, pick up a newspaper, or run an errand. Yet on the days he wore a suit and tie, Craig noticed he was never asked to do these odd jobs. He realized that running an errand wasn't asked of an executive with an important position and that when he looked like an executive, he was treated like one.

Upon this realization, Craig stopped dressing casually and started dressing as the other executives in the company did every day. Within a short amount of time, he was promoted. Craig has spent most of his career making sure he plays the part of the person he wants to be. Even now, as president of his own company, he believes his image plays a big role in his success.

Craig's experience isn't unusual; time and time again others have shared similar stories with me. The lesson: If you want others to notice you, do something noticeable. Whether you have your eyes set on a particular position or are interested in advancing as quickly as possible, you must demonstrate your ability and readiness. One of the easiest ways to do this is by *appearing* ready. This can be accomplished by dressing and acting as if you already are at the level you want to be.

COMPLICATIONS OF CASUAL CLOTHING

Dressing casually in the workplace ought to be considered a privilege, yet many people consider it to be the norm. Years ago, it would have been difficult to imagine going to work dressed in jeans, but today many people do. However, jeans are not considered typical business casual attire.

Many people mistakenly equate casual dress with casual activities, such as relaxing, running errands, exercising, and cleaning. However, a casual work environment is, and should be, different. Unless you are a laborer or work in manufacturing, T-shirts, jeans, and sweats are prohibited in most professional environments.

Although some people claim that dressing casually increases efficiency, I've had many managers tell me it decreases the decorum in an office. Many people believe that casual dress is here to stay, while others say it is on its way out. When people become too careless about their appearance, companies are forced to implement stricter clothing guidelines. I've seen it happen time and time again.

Employees typically enjoy dressing casually, but not all customers appreciate the relaxed attire. At times it is difficult to distinguish an employee in an office from a customer or delivery person, and, in a service establishment, this presents a problem if it is difficult to identify someone to assist you.

I was called in to help create and present new clothing guidelines to 400 employees of a bank after a valued customer closed her account. The reason: she didn't like discussing her financial matters with a person who looked as though he was ready to clean his garage. The customer was so offended by the appearance of the bank teller that she took her business elsewhere. She actually did the bank a favor by stating the reason she left, which drew attention to the potential pitfalls of employees dressing too casually.

What you wear often is dictated by customer expectations and the industry in which you work. The more conservative the industry, the more conservatively you'll need to dress. Young and creative companies have much more latitude when it comes to image and clothing. If you can't stand the thought of wearing a suit but you are in a career in a conservative industry, you need to realize that your *industry*——not your *preference*—dictates what you should wear. In traditional and conservative industries, conventional business attire is the norm.

It will be important for you to find out if there is a dress code in your workplace and if there are guidelines in place. Many companies assume employees know and understand what is acceptable attire and what is not, which may lead to some confusion about what is expected. Guidelines are helpful because they leave little to personal interpretation. Don't risk your reputation by dressing too casually or inappropriately. Pay close attention to what others are wearing, especially those in the positions you aspire for, and follow their lead.

FADS COME AND GO, BUT CLASSICS ARE FOREVER

Having raised three daughters, I am well aware of the importance many teens place on fads. I cannot tell you how often I have heard one of my daughters tell me that she *has to have* a certain piece of clothing or pair of shoes.

When it comes to dressing for an interview or your job, unless you are in the fashion industry, you don't have to worry about wearing the latest fad. You will want to look up to date, but understated is definitely better than overstated.

When you invest in classic clothing (clothing that doesn't go in and out of style), you don't have to worry about keeping up on the latest fashions, and you will be able to wear your clothes season after season.

As you begin to put together your work wardrobe, be patient. It can take years until you feel you have a solid wardrobe. When you make a purchase, select basic styles in the suits, jackets, slacks, shirts, and shoes you buy. Neutral, solid colors enable you to mix and match a garment with other pieces.

Think about it. A black pair of slacks can be worn a number of days in a week and paired with different jackets, shirts, or tops, and no one would know you were wearing the same slacks. However, if you wear a plaid jacket, not only will you have fewer options as to what to put with it, but because it is unique, it will be noticed and remembered.

The following styles are never recommended:

- **Oversized clothing.** Baggy pants riding below the waist may be a popular look, but there is nothing trendy about visible underwear or thongs—a consequence of wearing low cut pants. Loose-fitting clothing looks sloppy.

- **Undersized clothing.** Call it *undersized* or simply *too tight,* but don't pretend your clothes fit when they don't. Tight clothing draws attention to the body. The tighter something is, the more you risk appearing suggestive or, worse yet, unsightly.

- **Sweats.** Sweatpants and sweatshirts are much too casual to wear for work unless you work in a gym as a personal trainer.

- **T-shirts with slogans or graphics.** You may think the saying you're wearing is hysterical, but it could be offensive to someone else. Unless you are wearing a T-shirt with the company logo, don't promote any other business or manners of thinking.

- **Shorts.** If your company allows shorts, wear them, but wear them long; no shorter than two to three inches above your knees.

- **Miniskirts.** Skirts are fine as long as they aren't too short. Anything more than two or three inches above the knee is too short.

- **Sleeveless tops.** Even when it is warm outside, it isn't professional to expose too much skin. On women, sleeveless tops tend to reveal undergarments, which are supposed to be out of view. Many halter and tank tops are cut so low that cleavage is visible, which is unthinkable in a business environment.

- **Swimwear.** Obviously you know not to wear a swimsuit to work, but be sure you do not wear anything that resembles something you would wear on a hot, sunny day at the beach.

- **Loungewear.** Some loungewear resembles pajamas, and obviously pajamas are for sleeping, not for working. Loungewear enables you to lounge. Workplace attire enables you to work.

- **Vintage clothing.** Styles come and go; wearing something from a different era will make you look as though you are stuck in that era.

- **Headgear.** Hats, caps, and visors should never be worn for work unless it is part of a uniform.

ELIMINATE POTENTIAL BARRIERS

From the first interview until your last day on the job, the way you look impacts others and makes a statement about how you feel about yourself, your coworkers, and customers.

Select the clothing and styles that will help you achieve your objectives. If you are a photographer or artist or work in the fashion industry, what you wear won't matter as much as if you work in insurance, finance, or other conservative industries. Taking pride in your appearance shows you take pride in yourself and in your job and is one thing you *can* completely control. Consider the following as you put your look together:

Personal adornment has become increasingly popular and many people like to uniquely distinguish themselves with body art. Although more accepted now than in the past, some body art can be a distraction in the workplace and unknowingly prevent you from reaching your career goal. Think twice before you make the decision to decorate your body. The decisions you make today could become problems for you in the future.

Piercings

Pierced ears have always been fairly standard for women. However, wearing three or more earrings in one ear is not considered the norm. More men are wearing earrings now; however, if you are a male with pierced ears, think twice before showing up for an interview or work wearing earrings. Pierced noses, lips, and eyebrows are viewed more negatively than pierced ears. Unless you are certain your piercing won't be an issue, consider taking the rings out.

Tattoos

Tattoos can be distracting, offensive, or unattractive to others. One company I worked with had a strict policy about tattoos; anyone with visible tattoos had to cover them up. This meant that women with tattoos on their legs either had to wear pants or opaque tights so the tattoos would not show and men with tattoos on their arms were prohibited from wearing short sleeves.

You may not be able to do anything about tattoos you already have, but when making decisions about getting additional tattoos, consider placing them in inconspicuous areas. If you have visible tattoos, do what you can to cover them.

Jewelry

When it comes to wearing jewelry, the best rule of thumb is to keep it simple. Any type of noisy or gaudy jewelry is not recommended. Avoid extremely large earrings and keep the number of rings and bracelets you wear at one time to a minimum.

Cosmetics

If you are a woman, makeup that is carefully applied can enhance your appearance. However, be careful not to wear too much makeup and avoid wearing too much color. Select natural shades of makeup in neutral colors creating a natural, rather than made-up look.

Fragrance

Be wary of any fragrance you wear. What smells lovely to one person can be distasteful to another. The biggest mistake most people make when wearing fragrance is wearing too much of it. Your fragrance can induce an allergic reaction in someone else. Beware of hair and hygiene products with added fragrance that can clash with other products you are wearing. Overall, it is best to avoid wearing fragrance. If you want to smell good to others, opt for having no smell at all.

Personal Hygiene

You will likely at some time or another encounter someone with poor hygiene. Although it may be none of your business, it becomes your business when you are distracted or offended by someone else. Most people with poor hygiene have no idea how offensive they are to others. Few things are as embarrassing to talk about as personal hygiene, leaving those who need to know without a clue as to why others are avoiding them. Bathe frequently; use deodorant; wash your hose, undergarments, and clothing after wearing; and practice good oral hygiene.

PAY ATTENTION TO DETAIL: EVERYTHING GETS NOTICED

You might not think that anyone will notice the missing button on your jacket, the hole in the seam, or the stain on your shirt, but think again. Someone *will* notice and it might be the only thing remembered. Little things get noticed. Often it's the "problem" such as the stain or tear that is the *only* thing noticed because it stands out and draws attention.

Accidents happen; you lose a button, you spill something on yourself at lunch. It's the attention you pay to detail *every day* that counts. Be aware of the details you *can* control—the details that make a difference.

Shoes

You may think your shoes won't be noticed, but they will—especially in an interview. Polished shoes in good condition are a sign that you pay attention to detail. Keep your shoes in great condition by regularly cleaning and polishing them. Avoid wearing heels higher than three inches for ease in walking and standing. Do not wear dirty, worn-out sneakers or any footwear that you would wear for exercise. Unless you are given permission to wear sandals or go without socks, you will need to wear closed shoes. Sandals cover a wide range of styles, and while some may be acceptable, many are too casual and lack sufficient coverage for the workplace.

You want to be dressed well from head to toe. The shoes you wear can pull together or tear apart a professional look.

Socks

Socks are required. It doesn't matter if you'd rather go without; unless you are given permission to wear sandals or go without socks, you will need to wear socks. If you are allowed to go without socks, make sure your feet are in top condition. If your feet will be exposed at work, seriously consider treating yourself to a professional pedicure. Maintain the polish on your toenails, keep your toenails clean and neatly trimmed, and your heels in good condition; take care of rough or calloused heels.

Color

Color affects our moods and emotions. Each of us responds differently to colors. Not everyone will respond favorably to the bright orange and yellow striped slacks you wear, but no one will object—or notice—a neutral, solid-colored pair of pants. Build your wardrobe by purchasing suits, slacks, skirts, and jackets in neutral colors and accenting with other colors through blouses, shirts, scarves, and ties. In general, darker colors project confidence and strength. If you look very young, wearing darker colors can help you appear more mature. Lighter colors, which are softer to the eye, can make you appear more open and approachable.

Fabric

Pay attention to the fabric of a garment because it will determine how well something will wear. If the fabric looks wrinkled on the hanger, it will probably look wrinkled on you. You can test a garments fabric by the wrinkle test. Take a handful of the fabric in your hand and squeeze it tightly, then let it go. Is the fabric still wrinkled or did it smooth out? The way it looks after the wrinkle test is the way it will look on you when you wear it. You don't want to wear wrinkled clothing, so select fabrics that wear well.

Fit

One of the most important aspects of looking good is achieved by wearing clothing that fits properly. Avoid wearing clothing that is too tight or too loose; you need to be able to move, sit, and stand comfortably without exposing your undergarments or their outlines.

Cleanliness

The clothing you wear should be clean, free of spots or stains, well pressed and in good condition; no holes, rips, tears, or missing buttons. Use a lint brush to remove hair and lint from your clothing. Any item that is frayed or filled with little balls of fabric is not in good enough condition to wear to work. Wear clothing that is in top condition and do whatever you can to keep it that way.

Hair Style

A 2000 study directed by Yale University researcher Marianne LaFrance (and commissioned by Procter & Gamble), found that people make a variety of judgments about new acquaintances based on their hairstyles. The study reported that different hairstyles were found to create the following impressions:

- Women with short hair: perceived as confident and outgoing, but the least sexy.

- Women with long, straight, blonde hair: perceived as sexy, affluent, but narrow-minded.

- Women with medium-length, casually styled, dark hair: perceived as good-natured and intelligent.

- Men with short hairstyles: perceived as sexy, confident, but self-centered.

- Men with medium-length hair and a part on the side: perceived as intelligent, affluent, but narrow-minded.

- Men with long hair: perceived as good-natured, but also viewed as careless and unpleasant.

LaFrance also studied the effect of bad hair days on self-esteem. She found that when having a bad hair day, people felt less capable, less smart, and less sociable.

While there isn't one particular look to recommend, some hair-styles are more flattering and more mature looking than others. Consult with a good stylist about your hairstyle. The most important aspect of hair is that your haircut be maintained, and that your hair be clean, styled, and in good condition.

Hair Color

Coloring your hair in an unusual color is not recommended, nor is having the roots of your hair a different color from the rest of your hair. Both are very unflattering looks and unprofessional. Visit your stylist on a regular basis, touch up your color, and take care of your hair.

Facial Hair

Many men feel that facial hair enhances their features. If you fear your youthful looks are a disadvantage, facial hair can help you appear older. However, the "safest" look for professionals is to be clean-shaven.

Full beards are viewed less favorably than mustaches, partly because beards cover the face, making it difficult to see what lies beneath. Being able to view the expression on someone's face is important. If people can't "read" you, they may not understand you.

If you have facial hair, you will need to keep it neatly trimmed: don't let it grow too long or shaggy. Be especially careful when you eat, and make sure you don't have food in your mustache or beard. While facial hair is acceptable, hair in other places is often viewed negatively. Eliminate unwanted and unruly hair in your nose, ears, and eyebrows.

Obviously women don't choose to grow mustaches or beards, but some women do experience hair growth on their face and chest. Many women choose to remove the unwanted hair, but some do not. While light facial hair is common and not a problem for most women, dark hair is much more visible and is often considered unattractive. There are many permanent and temporary methods of hair removal. If facial hair is a problem for you, consider having it removed.

Hands

People notice your hands: You use them when you shake hands with someone, when exchanging business cards, and when writing, typing, speaking, and eating. Dry, chapped hands, ragged or bitten nails, hangnails, and dirty fingernails will be noticed and may send a negative message to others. If you bite your nails, try to break the habit. Not only will it be distracting if you bite them in front of others, but people who bite their nails may be considered nervous or anxious.

Extremely long and decorated nails are not the norm in the workplace and should be avoided. Fingernail polish is fine as long as you are not wearing fluorescent or other unusual colors and the nail polish is not chipped.

From the first interview until your last day on the job, the way you look makes a statement about how you feel about yourself, your coworkers, and customers. Many people mistakenly believe that once they have a job, it's safe to let their guard down. Assuming there is no need to impress anyone, they become remiss in their dress and, ultimately, their attitude. The way you look is just as important in an interview as it is every day thereafter. You might not care about your image, but other people do; project an image that will be an asset for you.

SUMMARY

Remember

✔ Your image matters. Dress better than you need to; dress for the position you want in the future, not the one you have today.

✔ Inquire about dress codes and ask for guidelines to help you in determining what to wear.

✔ Represent your company in the best possible manner. Every day, ask yourself, "What kind of impression do I want to make?" and select the clothing that will help you achieve your objective. Taking pride in your appearance shows you take pride in yourself and your job.

✔ You are better off being slightly overdressed than underdressed. Even if your job doesn't require it, dress better than you need to. People will notice and may treat you differently as a result. More importantly, you will look as though you take yourself and your job seriously, and you may find that your appearance creates the perception that you are ready to move up to the next level.

✔ Pay attention to detail. Make sure your clothing fits well, is clean, and is in good condition.

✔ When it comes to clothing and appearance, little things make a big difference. You can spend a lot of money on a garment, but if it is too tight, stained, or the lining hangs out, it will be distracting and cheapen your look.

✔ Build a long-lasting wardrobe of classic styles and neutral colors.

✔ Be patient as you build your work wardrobe. Purchase quality clothing in basic, classic styles and colors. This will enable you to mix and match pieces in your wardrobe and to wear your clothing for years without worrying about anything going out of style.

✔ Change your look every now and then, whether it's a new hairstyle or shaving the beard you've grown. You need to look as though you know what you are doing, so as things evolve and change, make some personal changes as well.

Chapter 9

Do's and Don'ts of Interviewing

CREATING YOUR WINNING IMPRESSION

Although many interviewers don't like to admit they make judgments quickly about job candidates, the reality is that most do. The initial glance and a handshake are about all it takes for someone to think they have a sense of who you are.

If you fail to make a good first impression, you decrease your chances for a second interview and your chances for a job offer. When there are a number of equally qualified candidates to choose from, an employer needs to have an efficient way to distinguish one candidate from another. Sometimes an interviewer will rely on his or her first impression or gut feeling about a job candidate and make a decision within the first few moments of an interview.

Making a positive impression starts with awareness of yourself and others. You need to think about many things in order to send the right message because *everything* you do or don't do will be noticed and evaluated. The following suggestions will help you make a positive impression from the moment you arrive until the interview comes to an end.

TONE OF VOICE

Have you ever sensed that someone was upset, yet when you asked if everything was okay the person replied, "I'm FINE," in a tone that contradicted his or her words? The manner in which you speak validates or invalidates what you say. When you greet someone and you say, "It's nice to meet you," do you sound sincere and truly happy to meet that person or does your tone and pitch detract from your sincerity?

Suggestion:

Speak enthusiastically and make sure the tone you speak with matches your words. For example, if you are talking about how enthused you are about something, *sound* enthused. You will also sound more interesting when you vary your tone and inflection throughout a conversation.

CHOICE OF WORDS

The words you use enable you to express what you are thinking and to build rapport with others. People expect you to have a command of the English language and to use a business vocabulary. You don't have to necessarily learn new words, but if a large part of your vocabulary is full of slang or jargon, you will sound as though you do not belong in a business environment. In addition, many people use fillers in their conversations by overusing "ums," "ahs," and "ers" in between words. A few fillers aren't usually noticed, but if you use them too often, it will be the *only* thing noticed.

Suggestion:

Work on building your vocabulary and avoid swearing and using slang, jargon, and fillers.

RATE OF SPEECH

Talking too fast or too slow can make you appear nervous. Notice the speech rate of newscasters and other people you find easy to listen to. When in conversation with someone, pay attention to that person's rate of speech and speak at a similar pace.

Suggestion:

If you tend to talk fast, slow down, and if you tend to speak too slowly, speed up.

ENUNCIATION

If you want people to understand you, you need to speak clearly. I used to go to a doctor who mumbled. I couldn't understand half of what he said, but I felt funny asking him for clarification repeatedly. I am certain that better communication skills would have benefited him and been appreciated by all of his patients.

Suggestion:

Listen to yourself on a tape recorder for an accurate appraisal of your enunciation and speech habits. Work at speaking clearly without mumbling.

VOLUME OF SPEECH

If you are too loud, you can appear rude. If you are too quiet, you risk appearing timid. Err on the side of loudness over quietness, but don't speak much louder than the person with whom you are conversing.

Suggestion:

Speak confidently and enthusiastically and try to match the volume of the person you are with, but don't be too boisterous.

ATTITUDE

It only takes a quick glance at someone to determine his or her attitude. A positive, confident, and enthusiastic attitude helps you make a great impression, and these qualities come from within.

Suggestion:

Even if you don't feel confident or enthusiastic, act as though you do. It may feel phony at first, but you will be surprised to discover that the way you act affects the way you feel.

GESTURES

Gestures are a natural means of expression and help us animate our conversations. Strong, bold gestures add impact to what we say while smaller gestures tend to reflect nervousness or anxiety.

Suggestion:

Be expressive. Use bold gestures to add interest to what you are saying.

HANDS

Your hands will be noticed; make sure your hands are well manicured. Keep your hands off of your hips, out of your pockets, and away from your face. One of the most powerful gestures is the steeple, which is created by holding your hands together with fingers straight and pointing up. If you don't know what to do with your hands, allow them to hang by your side or fold them together either in front of you or in your lap.

Suggestion:

Find a "home base" (your lap, a table, or a desk) to place your hands, but do use your hands as you are talking or to emphasize a point.

POSTURE

You don't want to slouch, but if you are too rigid, you risk appearing uncomfortable, too formal, or unapproachable. Always rise when you greet someone, and stand erect, with your shoulders back and head held high. When you are seated, sit upright with your feet touching the ground. If you have a choice between a hardback chair and a soft cushiony chair, choose the hardback. You will be in a better position to maintain good posture.

Suggestion:

In order to greet people confidently, stand tall and walk with a brisk, confident stride.

EXPRESSION

Are you aware of the expression on your face right now? You may be engrossed in this book, but if someone else were to see you, you might appear bored or even upset. It is important to vary your facial expressions in order to avoid being misread. Perhaps you've heard the expression, "A smile is worth a thousand words." A smile conveys friendliness in any language and is a wonderful business tool. Smiling helps you come across as friendly, approachable, and confident.

Suggestion:

Smile when you greet someone. Be aware of the expression on your face; vary your expression to avoid being misunderstood.

EYE CONTACT

Do you look at the person you are talking to? Eye contact is essential in building trust and should be maintained as much as possible when conversing with someone. When you fail to make eye contact with someone you risk appearing disinterested, dishonest, or unsure of yourself. If you are uncomfortable looking someone in the eyes, focus on their face or the bridge of their nose.

Suggestion:

Make a connection with your eyes and stay connected. When you are in conversation with someone, maintain eye contact at least 90 percent of the time.

GOOD MANNERS ARE AN ASSET

Manners will never go out of style and are an asset to anyone, especially in an interview. Displaying good manners conveys that you are well bred, respectful of others, and have the ability to blend with ease into a variety of environments.

Vault.com, a career content site, conducted a survey on interview manners in 2000. Employers were asked if they felt that manners had deteriorated in the interviewing and hiring process over the last few years.

Following are the results of the survey:

51%—Yes, they have

29%—Yes, a bit

17%—Not very much

3%—Not at all

Interviewers have to put up with a lot, but the survey shows they do have their limits. The following percent of employers would automatically reject otherwise qualified candidates who indulged in the following behaviors during an interview:

95% would disqualify for making a cell phone call

89% for leaving before the interview is over

86% for accepting a cell phone call

86% for bringing a pet

85% for removing shoes

77% for exhibiting poor hygiene

76% for asking for a cigarette break

74% for using profanity

61% for applying or reapplying lipstick

60% for bringing a child

30% for arriving 10 minutes or more late

27% for taking longer than a 10-minute bathroom break

10% for arriving 30 minutes or more early

4% for removing a jacket

An employer who participated in the survey related the following story: "A male stripped down to the buff in the parking lot in full view of hundreds of offices and changed into his interview suit. I received a dozen phone calls warning me that he was on his way to my office. I barely kept a straight face in the interview."

The lesson: From the moment you pull into the company parking lot or enter the building where the company is located, you are being scrutinized. Assume eyes are on you, because they probably are. For starters, make sure your car is clean and in good condition. If you pull up and your car is rumbling or noisy you may draw attention to yourself in the same way you would if you were dropped off at the door in a limousine. Neither would help you to make a very good first impression.

Everyone you encounter could influence your job potential. Smile, say hello, and be friendly and respectful to the door person, the receptionist, the secretary, and anyone with whom you come into contact. Many interviewers rely on others' opinion of a job candidate, so make sure you make a good impression with *everyone*.

TIPS FOR INTERVIEW SUCCESS

An interview can be stressful, but it doesn't have to be. The following tips will help you prepare for interview success:

- **Confirm the date and time.** Make sure you have the right date, time, and place of the interview by repeating the information when you schedule it and writing it down in a secure place. Get the name of the person you will be meeting with and that person's phone number.

- **Get a good night's sleep.** You don't want to be sleepy; people have dozed off during an interview—not a wise thing to do! Get plenty of rest, try not to yawn, and be as alert and energized as possible.

- **Reschedule if you are sick.** If you have a cold and can take medication that will stop the sneezing and blowing of your nose, then do so. If you risk a coughing attack, then bring a lozenge with you, but it is much easier to talk without anything in your mouth. However, if you are running a fever or have the stomach flu, do yourself and everyone else a favor and stay home.

- **Dress to impress.** Don't worry about being overdressed if the company permits casual attire. You are a visitor—not an employee of the company. You are unemployed and must do everything you can to look as though you really want the job. Wear a suit or something comparable that is clean, fits well, and in top condition. Remember: Interviewers look at the shoes of candidates to find out who pays attention to detail; polish your shoes and be sure they are in top condition.

- **Be prepared.** Bring a professional-looking notepad and pen and test the pen to make sure it works. Carry a professional looking briefcase or portfolio that is in good condition and make sure it is neatly organized, removing anything you will not need.

- **Be on time.** Plan on arriving at least 15 minutes early. This will give you time to find a place to park, visit the rest room, and relax before you are ushered in for the interview. However, don't arrive *too* early (30 minutes or more), or you risk appearing too eager for the job and it may seem as though you have nothing better to do with your time.

- **Turn off your phone.** The last thing you want is to have your phone ringing or vibrating in the middle of an interview. Consider leaving your phone in the car. However, if you must have it with you, check and double check to make sure it is turned *off*. If your phone rings despite your efforts to turn it off, apologize, silence the ringing, then turn the phone off.

- **Don't smell.** Come clean to an interview. Take a shower and wash your hair. Air out your clothing, especially if you smoke, and brush and floss your teeth. You definitely don't want to smell like cigarette smoke (a real turn-off for most people), but trying to mask it with cologne is a big mistake. The fragrance you're so fond of could offend someone else or cause an allergic reaction, which will likely bring your interview to an abrupt end. No scent is the only scent for an interview.

- **Be the first to offer a handshake**. Don't wait for someone else to reach their hand out to you. Be the first to reach out to others, both at the beginning and at the end of an interview. Firmly grip the other person's hand; you don't want to squeeze hard enough to cause pain, but you don't want your hand to be limp either. Practice shaking with others (before you go out on an interview) and ask for feedback about your handshake.

- **Wait for direction before you sit down.** Don't rush to sit down or select the most comfortable-looking chair to sit in. Allow the interviewer to show you where to sit.

- **Listen attentively**. Have intelligent questions prepared and engage in conversation, but never interrupt the interviewer or monopolize the conversation. Be a good listener and respond at the appropriate time.

- **Remain calm and in control**. Stand tall, shoulders back, hold your head high, look the interviewer in the eyes, smile, and don't forget to breathe—slowly. You may be surprised to discover that by doing these things you will calm your nerves and appear more confident and in control.

- **Be Still.** Don't fidget; it's a dead giveaway that you are nervous. Refrain from playing with your hair, fidgeting with your jewelry, tapping your fingers, or swinging your leg. Keep your hands still when not in use.

- **Use formal titles**. Always address the interviewer by his or her surname or formal title unless you are invited to use his or her first name. It's better to start out more formally than it is for you to assume it is acceptable to be on a first-name basis. And, make sure you understand the name so you pronounce it correctly.

- **Do not eat, chew gum, or smoke.** Do not eat, chew, or suck on anything during the interview. Never smoke before (or you'll reek of cigarette smoke), during, or immediately after an interview until you are no longer on the premises.

- **Have copies of your resume and references with you.** Always carry your resume with you because you never know who or how many people you might be meeting. Be prepared to provide additional information such as personal references and names and numbers of previous employers.

- **Know what is on your resume.** Make sure you know what's on your resume. It is not uncommon for an interviewer to ask you about your job history, so be prepared to talk about it.

- **Emphasize the positive.** Emphasize your qualities and positive traits. Never badmouth previous employers, complain about past experiences or your current job, or speak negatively about other people.

- **Ask questions.** Ask intelligent questions about the position and the company, etc., but don't ask about salary, vacation, sick days, or about anything that might indicate you are more interested in the perks of the job than the job itself.

- **Speak with conviction.** Beware of speech habits that can undermine your intentions. Don't question your ability or speak wishfully by saying, *"I hope," "I think," or "I'll try."* Be affirming and say, *"I know," "I am," "I will," "I can."*

- **Be truthful.** Even a little white lie can get you into big trouble. As long as you tell the truth you will never have to worry about keeping your story straight. If you don't know the answer to a question, it is better to admit it and say you will find out than to answer incorrectly.

- **Say thank you.** Always thank the interviewer for his or her time. Send a handwritten thank you note, reiterating your interest in the position within 24 hours of the interview.

- **Smile:** A sincere smile will lighten up the tension in your face and help you to appear friendly, approachable, and relaxed. Beware of overdoing the smile—as long as it is sincere and used appropriately it can be one of your most valuable interviewing tools.

THE EFFECTIVE EXIT

There will be a time in the interview when the momentum will slow down a bit. You may be asked if you have any more questions, and if you do not, it may be the beginning of the end of the interview. The signal that the interview is coming to an end may be less overt; the interviewer may begin to gather papers or close the folder with your information. He or she may simply stand up, signaling that it is time for you to leave.

When the interview is over, gracefully stand up, express your desire for the position, and determine the next step. For example, is there any additional information the interviewer needs? When is a decision anticipated? Would a follow-up call be appropriate? Then thank the interviewer for his or her time, extend your hand for a farewell handshake, and say good-bye.

This is not the time to throw in the question you forgot to ask or change your interview behavior. Your exit is just as important as your entrance. You want to make a great first impression and leave a positive, lasting impression.

WHEN THE INTERVIEW IS ON THE PHONE

Not every interview you have will be in person; some of your interviews might be conducted over the telephone. If you have a telephone interview scheduled, treat it as you would a face-to-face interview, but be aware of some of the challenges when interviewing by phone. Because you can't see the interviewer, it is more difficult to get a sense of how he or she is responding to you. However, if you put forth extra effort, you should be able to come across well, accomplish your objectives, and conduct a successful interview.

Consider a phone interview equally as important as a face-to-face interview. Be prepared; have your resume in front of you, information about the company, questions you want to ask, and a pen and notepad for notes. One advantage of telephone interviewing is that you can glance at your notes, so jot down a few key points you want to make or questions you want to remember to ask. However, don't overuse them or you risk sounding canned; you want to stay involved in the conversation and respond authentically.

Be ready a few minutes early and conduct the interview in a quiet place, preferably a room with a door that you can close. Alert others that you are going to be on the phone so that they can accommodate your need for quiet. If necessary, put a "do not disturb" sign on your door to inform others.

Do what you can to eliminate all background noise: Close windows, turn off all other phones and call waiting; turn off your computer, the television, the radio, and anything else that might interfere with the interview.

Be especially aware of your speech and tone of voice when on the phone, making sure you speak clearly and directly into the mouthpiece. Do not use a speakerphone for your telephone interview and, when possible, speak on a land phone rather than a cell phone to ensure the best possible connection. Just as you shouldn't eat, chew gum, or smoke when having an interview in person, you should refrain from doing these things during a telephone interview as well. Nor should you talk with others, take another call, use the computer, or shuffle through papers during your phone interview. No matter how discreet you try to be, these things can be heard over the phone and will be irritating to the person with whom you are interviewing. Do keep a glass of water nearby should you need to moisten your throat or prevent a coughing attack.

JOB FAIRS

The people you meet and interviews you have at a job fair are just as important as other types of interviews, so prepare as you would for any other type of interview. Even if you attend with a friend, you are better off separating once you get there and meeting people individually.

- Dress professionally; dress for a job fair as you would any other type of interview. Walk around the job fair before you begin working it. Get a feel for the layout and identify the location of those companies in which you are most interested.

- Introduce yourself and include a brief explanation of who you are and what you have to offer an organization. This brief intro should be prepared in advance.

- Be respectful of others. Give others privacy and never interrupt a conversation.

- Wait patiently for your turn to speak with someone, but don't wait too long. You are better off coming back to a table that has a long line of people waiting.

- Know something about the companies you talk with. This should be done in advance, but if not, take some company literature from the table and read it before you introduce yourself.

- Bring plenty of copies of your resume; you're better off having more than you need than risking running out and not having enough to hand out.

- Carry a briefcase big enough to hold the information you gather. Do take business cards and literature the companies offer.

- Make notes about the conversations you have and with whom. Having a number of conversations makes it difficult to remember specific details, so take the time to jot down notes about the organization or people you met.

- Talk with as many people as you can. Make a personal introduction when handing out your resume rather than leaving resumes on tables; you have a much better chance of being remembered.

- Check your coat if you wore one; you do not want to appear as though you are breezing through in a hurry.

- Be brief. You don't want to drop off your resume and dash, but you don't want to overstay your welcome or monopolize anyone's time. Conversations at job fairs are meant to be brief; respect the needs of the employers and other job seekers.

- Talk with other job seekers. You can learn a lot of valuable information by talking with others—even those who are there looking for jobs.

- Follow up. As with any other type of interview, if someone took his or her time to meet with you, send a thank you note within 24 hours and follow up after that.

INTERVIEWING OVER A MEAL

Some companies won't even consider hiring or promoting someone until a company representative and the person have dined together. Table manners are important and reveal a lot about a person. If you are being considered for a position, one of your interviews could be over a meal. If you don't watch your table manners, someone else will.

Embarrassing things can happen when you are eating, talking, and trying to maintain a sense of control. Food can become lodged in your teeth, strings of cheese may hang from your mouth, utensils may drop on the floor, and something is bound to spill; expect the unexpected. Not one of these things will dismiss you as a candidate for a job; however, your reaction to these events is what people will notice and, as a result, judge you on.

If you typically eat in front of the television, slurp your soup, gobble down a meal within five minutes and think that the louder the belch, the bigger the compliment to the chef, it will be difficult for you to put on the charm when you need to. Learn by observing others and by practicing good habits every day.

IDEAS TO CHEW ON

Keep the following tips in mind when you are dining:

- Place your napkin on your lap immediately after being seated and keep it on your lap until you get up to leave, and then place it neatly on the table.

- When deciding what to order, choose something easy to eat. Avoid triple-decker sandwiches, spaghetti, or any food that requires skill and focus.

- If you are unsure about what to order, ask what your host recommends.

- If you are unsure about which plate or glass to use, observe what others are doing.

- If you are unsure which utensil to use, observe what others are doing or work from the outside of your silverware setting in.

- If you need to leave the table during the meal, simply say, "Excuse me," and place your napkin on the chair.

- If you have special dietary needs, be discreet when discussing them and don't make a big issue about it.

- Wait to begin eating until everyone has been served or until you've been invited to eat by others who have not yet been served.

- Do not pick your teeth or use a toothpick at the table.

- Learn the proper way to hold and use your utensils. Never shovel food into your mouth.

- Taste your food before adding salt or pepper (you don't want to appear as though you make rash decisions) and wait to see if others use steak sauce or ketchup before you use it.

- If you need something passed to you, ask for it rather than reaching across the table to get it.

- If someone asks for the salt, pass the pepper, too.

- Avoid commenting on others' food, prices, or the bill.

- If your beverage comes in a can or bottle, request a glass.

- Do not talk with your mouth full of food.

- Dab, rather than wipe, your face with the napkin provided.

- Do not put lipstick on at the table.

- Do not blow your nose at the table.

- Don't burp.

- Do not smoke.

- Do not drink alcohol.

SUMMARY

Remember:

✔ Think about what kind of impression you want to make and make a plan to accomplish your objective.

✔ Look good. Wear a suit and pay attention to other appearance details; make sure your hair is clean and styled, your clothing clean and pressed, and your shoes shined.

✔ Exude confidence. Stand tall, sit upright, hold your head high, shoulders back, and walk with vigor.

✔ Radiate friendliness. Greet everyone (including the receptionist) with warmth.

✔ Be positive. Do not talk badly about yourself, other people, or complain about anything. Develop an optimistic mind-set and an upbeat attitude and you will have an advantage over those who are self-doubting.

✔ Listen. Be a good listener and a good conversationalist, but don't talk too much or monopolize the conversation.

✔ Extend yourself. Offer a firm, strong handshake at the beginning and end of an interview.

✔ Smile. Smile when you greet someone and even when you are talking with someone on the phone. A smile can be seen and heard and will help you appear friendlier and in control; share your smile with everyone you greet.

✔ Make eye contact. Maintain eye contact during your interview, glancing away occasionally, but always remaining focused on the person with whom you are talking.

✔ Gesture naturally. Find a home base for your hands and let your gestures add interest to your conversation.

✔ Display respect. Don't use first names unless you are asked to, rise when you greet someone, and be a good listener.

✔ Be mindful of good manners. Turn off your cell phone and do not eat, chew gum, smoke, or wear fragrance.

✔ Be gracious. Thank the interviewer for his or her time and handwrite and mail a thank you note within one business day.

Chapter 10

The Interview Is Over: Now What?

AFTER THE INTERVIEW

When the interview is over you'll probably feel a sense of relief—and you should; interviews can be stressful. However, resist the temptation to start celebrating or take off for the rest of the day, because what you do after the interview is just as important as what you do before and during an interview.

It is important to evaluate your performance after the interview is over. You can do this in your car, at a coffee shop, or when you get home, but whatever you do, do it as soon as possible upon leaving the interview site. Jot down on paper anything and everything you remember about the interview, including information the interviewer shared. You might think you will remember what was said, but chances are you will not remember everything, which is why it is important to write it down.

Next, evaluate your performance. How do you think the interview went? What do you like best about how it went; what did you do especially well and what do you want to do differently next time? Are you pleased with the way you answered questions? Do you ask the right questions? Do you feel you were prepared? If not, what do you need to do next time to be better prepared? Ask yourself, did I remember to express interest in the position, ask about the timeframe in which a decision will be made, and determine the next step? Did I remember to ask for the job? Did I remember to get business cards of the people I met? Save the cards, and write down the correct name and contact information.

The time to assess an interview is when it is fresh in your mind. Evaluating your performance will help you determine points to include in follow-up correspondence and prepare you to be even more effective in future interviews. Don't overlook this important step.

SEND A THANK YOU NOTE

One of the easiest ways to increase your chances of serious consideration after a job interview is by writing and sending a thank you note. Although this is the expected protocol, many job seekers underestimate the value of expressing thanks this way and therefore skip this important step.

While some people will tell you sending a thank you by e-mail should suffice, others will tell you that nothing is as effective or impressive as a hand-written thank note. While e-mail is more efficient, a handwritten note is more personal. If you are not comfortable writing a note, generating a letter by computer is fine, but unless you know that the person's preferred method of correspondence is through the Internet, put in the extra effort to mail your thank you note or letter within one business day of the interview—the sooner you get your note out, the better.

Surprisingly, many people underestimate the value of a thank you note. This little act can make a *big* difference, and sometimes is the determining factor when deciding between two candidates. It doesn't take much time to write a thank you note, and it may be the crucial factor that sets you apart from other candidates.

You don't need to write a lengthy note, and there is some debate over whether typed or handwritten notes are preferred. Studies have shown that executives will open hand-addressed envelopes before opening computer-generated labels or typed envelopes.

Think about the mail you receive. What types of letters do you open first? If you are like most people, it's not the bills or solicitations you receive, but rather anything that is hand addressed that probably catches your attention and is opened first. And, because we don't receive much handwritten correspondence anymore, it has greater appeal. However, if you choose to handwrite a thank you note, be sure to write legibly. A thank you note has many benefits and helps you to:

- Show an understanding of employer expectations and business protocol.

- Display courtesy.

- Demonstrate communication skills.

- Distinguish yourself from other candidates.

- Reinforce your interest in the position.

- Remind the interviewer of your relevant skills and qualifications.

- Clarify points discussed in the interview.

- Add anything you forgot to say in the interview.

- Keep your name in front of decision makers.

- Establish expectations for the next step, demonstrating initiative and follow through.

The most important aspect of a thank you note is writing it and getting it to the person who interviewed you as quickly as possible. Take advantage of this additional opportunity to sell yourself one more time as the best person for the job. However, be careful not to overdo it. The following are guidelines to consider when crafting a thank you:

- Write legibly. If your handwriting isn't legible, use the computer.

- Make it brief and to the point.

- Use a professional, yet personal tone.

- Check spelling and grammar to make sure it is error free.

- Thank the person for interviewing you and for expressing interest in you.

- Be affirmative.

- Emphasize your strengths and why you are a good fit for the position.

- Recap the interview.

- State your interest in both the organization and the position.

- Provide any information the employer requested or important information you forgot to mention in the interview.

THANKS, BUT NO THANKS

A thank you note shows that you understand protocol; it validates your interest in the position and demonstrates initiative. In a 2000 survey, Vault.com asked employers what, if any, impact the thank you note had on a candidate's chances of getting hired. They responded as follows:

36% It always helps.

42% It helps when deciding between two or more candidates.

22% It does not matter.

Employers were then asked how often they receive thank you notes from candidates. Their responses were as follows:

0%   100% of the time

10% 75-99% of the time

26% 50-74% of the time

20% 25-49% of the time

36% 1-24% of the time

8%   Nobody sends thank you notes anymore.

TO CALL OR NOT TO CALL?

Whether or not you should follow up with a phone call will be based somewhat on the final conversation you had at the interview. If, when determining your next step, the interviewer specifically told you not to call, then don't. If, however, it was left open as to who will follow up with whom, or if nothing was said, you can and should follow up with a phone call within one week.

With each conversation you have, determine the "next step," and continue to follow up if you are encouraged to do so, but be careful not to become a pest. Really listen to what the interviewer is telling you. You want to appear interested and persistent, but you need to know when to back off, and you never want to appear desperate.

Above all, try to talk with the person directly when you call and avoid leaving too many voicemail messages. If you find it necessary to leave a message, know what you plan on saying before you call. You don't want to leave a long, rambling message—you are trying to impress, not irritate, the person you are calling. It can help to write out what you want to say before you call, and if you do, be sure you don't sound as though you are reading it when you speak.

THE WAITING GAME

One of the most difficult aspects of the job search is waiting. A big mistake for job seekers is to sit back and wait for the phone to ring or an offer to come through. Don't put your life, or your job search, on hold while you wait for a decision to be made. Doing so won't make a company move any faster to make a hiring decision.

No matter how badly you want a position or how perfectly suited you feel you are for a particular position, never stop looking or interviewing until you have received and accepted an offer. Even when a job offer appears imminent, there's a chance it won't come through. You can't afford to lose your momentum; never count on an offer that hasn't been made.

Don't wait for others to get back to you. Keep in touch with those you are waiting on, keep your job search going, and keep your options open.

You should continue to make contact with the people and companies you are interested in and that express interest in you, but be sure to put your time and energy toward the most viable opportunities.

I realize the most important thing to you is to know where you stand with a company. Waiting and wondering is not easy, but don't expect closure with every aspect of your job search. It would be ideal if companies got back to every interviewee it had, but the reality is that most companies do not. Sometimes people will lead you on because they don't want to disappoint or reject you; sometimes there are so many candidates it becomes too time consuming, and expensive, to contact them all. If you can get closure, it's great, but it is unlikely that you will. At some point you need to draw your own conclusion and give up your hopes of hearing from someone who hasn't responded to you. Focus on those who are responsive instead.

DEALING WITH REJECTION

If there's one thing you can count on, it's being rejected. Rare is the person who never experiences rejection. One of the easiest ways to prepare for rejection is to expect it. When you do, it won't come as an unexpected or painful surprise. Some rejection is to be anticipated; however, if you are rejected repeatedly for jobs you know you are qualified for, it is important to evaluate the reason.

If you are getting your resume out and not receiving requests for interviews, reevaluate your resume and your submission strategy, because one or both are not working for you. A good resume sent to the right people will generate interviews.

If you are going on interviews, but not being asked back for a second interview or receiving any offers, you need to work on your interviewing and presentation skills. Seek input from someone who can give you an objective and unbiased opinion about what you are or are not doing that could be hindering your progress.

When you are rejected, try not to take it too personally, because it usually isn't a personal affront. When someone else is selected for a job instead of you, it doesn't imply you aren't good enough—it's likely that someone else was better suited for the job.

The healthiest way to deal with rejection is to appreciate it, realizing that it wasn't meant to be. It is worth waiting for the right fit, and chances are a better opportunity will come. I realize it can be difficult to stay positive when you have been rejected repeatedly, but as long as you keep evaluating yourself, learning from each experience, and working on improving your interviewing and presentation skills, there is no reason to be down on yourself. It may take you longer than someone else to find a job, but it doesn't have anything to do with the value you bring to a company or your future success. Everyone's path is different; don't compare yourself to others, and don't take rejection too personally.

YOU'RE HIRED

The time will come when you will receive your first job offer. Hearing "You're hired" may be music to your ears, but don't rush to accept the first offer—or any offer you get. Be appreciative of the offer and express your enthusiasm, but make sure you know what is being offered before you accept and give yourself time to make a well thought-out decision.

Accepting a job is a big commitment and one you shouldn't take lightly. Before you accept, make sure you have a clear understanding of your job responsibilities and the package being offered. The best way to do that is to get the offer in writing, which the company will likely do and is something you can request.

Not every offer will include everything you seek in a job, making it important for you to determine the difference between what you need and what you want. When contemplating an offer, consider the entire package being presented so that you can make an informed decision.

If you choose to decline an offer, don't delay. Be respectful of the company's need to move on without you. Inform your contact of your decision by phone, then follow up with a statement in writing. Be professional and respectful, doing everything you can to leave a positive impression and the door open for future opportunities.

SUMMARY

Remember:

✔ Evaluate every job interview. Take the time to evaluate your performance immediately after every interview you have. Identify the things you did well and the areas you need to improve.

✔ Get business cards from the people you meet and be sure you have the correct name and contact information of the person who interviews you.

✔ Write and send a thank you note within 24 hours of your job interview.

✔ Call to check in with the person who interviewed you about a week after the interview.

✔ Determine the next step after each conversation.

✔ Be persistent, but don't be a pest.

✔ Don't take rejection personally.

✔ Take some time before accepting a job offer to evaluate it and make a well-thought-out decision.

Chapter 11

When You're the Newcomer

YOUR FIRST DAY

When the moment you've been waiting for has arrived and you are about to experience the first day of your first *real* job, you are to be congratulated. This is an exciting time for you and a pivotal time in your life.

You may be under the assumption that all of the preparation, learning, studying, and test taking you've endured to get to this point is behind you now. Perhaps you feel fully prepared for what lies ahead. I hope you are, but as you begin your new job and jump-start your career, don't forget that you are embarking on what is sure to be one of the largest learning curves you've had yet.

You might even find, as you get ready for your first day of work, that it reminds you of the way you used to feel on the first day of school. There was always something special about that first day: the anticipation of a new teacher, the hope of making new friends, and the chance for a fresh start with a clean slate.

As you prepare for your first day of work, this, too, is a new beginning. You will be meeting new people, entering a new environment, and adjusting to a different schedule.

It might help make the transition easier if you view your first job as an extension of your education. On the first day and for an extended period of time at your new job, you will be in a learning mode. Be prepared to listen and ask questions. You may even feel inadequate at times. If so, don't worry; it's all part of the learning process.

PLAYING THE PART OF A PROFESSIONAL

You don't have to be an actor to appreciate a great performance. There is a reason some of the best actors are paid millions of dollars; they do more than act—they *become* the person in the role they are playing. Each new role an actor plays requires a change in appearance and behavior.

If you were the director of a play and had to advise the young lead actor how to "play the part" of a professional in a typical business environment, what advice would you give?

If the lead were male, would you suggest he wear a suit and tie? What about a female? Would you tell her to wear a miniskirt or a pantsuit? What details would be necessary to make the character believable? How would you direct the actors as they try to "act" professional? Which mannerisms would they need to capture?

Think of your new position as a role you're about to play. *You* are the director of this new role you are "playing." How will *you* look and act?

YOUR NEW ROLE: LOOKING THE PART OF A PROFESSIONAL

You've accepted a role to play; now you need to determine how to perform your best. The way you look is crucial in determining how believable you will be in your new role. For your first day, select something that represents you well, keeping in mind you will be meeting many people for the first time.

Whether consciously or unconsciously, each of us sends a message about who we are every time we interact with another person. Making sure you convey the appropriate message is important in establishing your credibility, no matter what role you are playing. And, since the clothing you wear is noticed before anything else, it's important to wear clothing that reflects your desired message.

As the newcomer, each person you meet is going to be assessing you, wondering what you're all about. Initially the only information to go on is how you *appear.* Do you look and act like somebody who can do the job, not only the job you have now but the one you are striving for?

Take time to think about and create your new look. You don't need to give up your individuality in order to look the part of the role you are playing. There is plenty of room within the bounds of appropriateness for you to create a look that you and others will be comfortable with. Evaluate and carefully plan for this new role you have assumed, and then do what's necessary to reinforce it every single day.

ACTING THE PART OF A PROFESSIONAL

Once you've got the look, you need to think about how you will be expected to *act*. What actions and mannerisms are expected of someone in the role you are playing? Chances are you worked hard to get this job. You thought carefully about how you wanted to present yourself in the interview. Now, all you need to do is to keep it up; whatever you did worked for you.

You will want people to feel comfortable in your presence. Developing the skill of making others feel comfortable will pay off in the long run. People who are at ease (and put others at ease) in a variety of situations are viewed positively. Do you act like someone your coworkers, boss, and customers can work well with? Do you appear approachable and friendly?

Your actions are derived from what you say and, even more importantly, *how* you say things. The way you carry yourself, your gestures, facial expressions, and mannerisms all communicate much about you. Perhaps you've heard the expression, "A picture is worth a thousand words." Your "picture" is how you appear to others and says far more about you than words could possibly say. Create in your mind the picture of someone perfectly playing your role and then become that person. Act the part of a professional.

BEING THE PART OF A PROFESSIONAL

As you begin playing your new role, it may feel forced or even phony, but if you continue to pursue these new behaviors, they will become a part of who you are. Do you look and act trustworthy? Are you the type of person others can depend upon? Most importantly, are you consistent? Can others depend on you to be this way every day? Consistency is the key. Be the kind of person you want to be and you will not only play the part of a professional but you will become one. If you were an actor in a play, would you skip rehearsals and hope for your performance to come together opening night?

You are about to take on your biggest new role yet. You want to give your best performance. No actor ever received a standing ovation without first planning and preparing for his or her role. How will you succeed if you don't plan and prepare for your new role?

Plan who you want to be and where you want to go. On your first day on the job, when you are the newcomer, look, act, and be consistent in the role you have accepted; be the professional you want to be. Your efforts will pay off. People will respond positively toward you and you will have a great experience your first day and, hopefully, every day thereafter.

MAKING A GOOD IMPRESSION ON YOUR FIRST DAY AND EVERY DAY

You will be meeting many new people and you will want to make a positive first impression with everyone you meet. Although first impressions are made rather quickly and based on initial judgments, the effects are long lasting.

What kind of impression do you want to make your first day on the job? It is important to decide because the way you present yourself initially will leave long-lasting impressions on the people you meet. Therefore, it will help if you make these decisions *before* you get to work.

How do you want to come across to others? Let's assume you want to appear friendly, confident, and professional. What do you think you will need to do to communicate friendliness, confidence, and professionalism? Let's take a look at each one individually:

Friendly: In order to appear friendly you have to be open and responsive to everyone you meet. You'll want to be comfortable with yourself, make others feel comfortable around you, and appear interested in what others have to say.

Confident: You may not feel as confident as you'd like when you are the newcomer, but you can appear more confident than you feel. Start by reminding yourself that you were offered this job because others have confidence in you. Next, remind yourself of the reasons you believe in yourself. Then take a deep breath, stand tall, hold your head high, and look directly at the people you meet. Doing this will help you project a sense of confidence, self-reliance, and comfort.

Professional: Consider the culture of the organization as you decide what to wear on your first day, and every day. Select clothing to wear that is flattering and appropriate for work. Be aware of your surroundings and respectful of others; don't draw unnecessary attention to yourself by talking too loudly or by disturbing others in any way.

The following are additional tips for making a favorable impression as the newcomer:

- **Be on time.** Better yet, be early. Plan for and anticipate possible problems in advance. You don't have enough experience yet to gauge the traffic, parking, and other factors involved with getting to work, so leave plenty of time for delays. You will be much more relaxed and make a better impression if you arrive early.

- **Introduce yourself.** If others don't introduce themselves to you, introduce yourself to them. Acknowledge the people you see and let people know who you are. It will make you, and others, more comfortable and help you to make a positive first impression.

- **Smile.** It may sound simplistic, but smiling is hardly simple. Many people take themselves and their work too seriously.

People like to deal with people, not robots. A smile speaks volumes. A smile generally is received positively and then returned, communicating a positive message or "vibe" between the parties exchanging smiles. You don't want to walk around with a frozen or phony smile on your face, but do smile at those you greet and be aware of your expression throughout the day.

- **Offer a handshake.** Once you get into the routine of coming to work each day it won't be necessary to shake hands with everyone you see each time you see them. But on the first day, as you are introduced to others, extend your hand to everyone you meet. This will help you establish yourself as a friendly and outgoing new employee. Make sure your grip is firm and strong.

- **Make eye contact.** When you meet someone, look into their eyes long enough to remember their eye color. This usually amounts to about four to six seconds and is substantially longer than the one- to three-second glance we typically give someone upon being introduced. Prolonged eye contact helps you to connect with another individual and enables you to appear sincere when you say, "It's nice to meet you."

- **Remember names.** You will be meeting a number of people, and although it will be easier for others to remember your name because you are the one who is new, you will really make an impression if you remember the names of everyone you meet. One way to remember a name is through repetition. Use the name in conversation shortly after you hear it. You may want to associate the name with something or even write it down for reinforcement.

- **Ask questions.** Your employer will have many spoken and unspoken expectations about you. Make sure you understand these expectations and if you are unsure about something, ask for clarification. Wondering or guessing will only create confusion. Asking questions shows you desire to do well and you are interested in fitting into your new environment. It also prevents misunderstandings that could lead to future problems.

- **Be enthusiastic.** If you are enthused about your first day, it will be contagious to others. Show your enthusiasm through your positive attitude, your desire to learn, and your ability to listen.

- **Be humble.** The last thing you want to do is to begin your new job with a know-it-all, overly confident attitude. Your attitude will be an asset as long as you have the *right* attitude. Remember, you're the newcomer; no one expects you to know it all, so no matter how much you think you know, keep it to yourself. Be humble.

- **Be committed.** Be committed to making this job work out. Your commitment will sustain you and make you less likely to become disillusioned when problems arise. Without a strong sense of commitment, little things are difficult to overlook, and you may be more likely to leave if things don't work out as you planned.

THE UNWRITTEN, UNSPOKEN EXPECTATIONS

Both you and your employer have expectations of each other. Although you may not feel the need to discuss each and every expectation you have with your supervisor once you are employed, the fact is that they do exist.

You probably assume your employer will:

- Pay you
- Pay you on time
- Respect you
- Listen to you
- Train you

- Offer benefits

- Allow breaks during the day

- Conduct reviews

- Give pay raises

- Provide a desk, computer, and other tools to help you do your job

You may have other expectations that are not listed. Think about what you expect. Your employer has expectations, too, many of which are often implied, not spoken.

Your employer is counting on you to:

- Work hard each business day

- Arrive on time

- Assert yourself and take initiative to get things done

- Have a positive attitude

- Communicate clearly

- Get along with coworkers

- Look good

- Act professionally

- Do what you say

- Be dedicated to your job

- Be dependable

- Be honest and trustworthy

These are just some of the expectations your employer has; however, there may be many more. You will never know unless you ask; it is difficult to meet expectations if you don't know what they are. Think about how you might feel if your employer missed a pay period or failed to live up to any of your other expectations. You probably would not be very happy. Even though your employer may never specifically tell you some of the things that are expected, it doesn't mean the expectations don't exist.

It is important for you to identify the expectations of your employer to make sure you live up to those standards. When you are offered a job, you can assume that you have met most of the expectations your employer had for the person who would fill your position.

YOUR EMPLOYER'S GREATEST FEARS

A business executive who requested anonymity had this to say about today's young professionals: "The number-one problem I've seen with employees fresh out of college is their inability to grasp the concepts of coming to work at the established time, coming to work every day, and having backup plans when there are daycare issues, traffic problems, or weather problems. The idea of leaving for work a little early when the radio reports traffic backed up or weather problems just does not occur to them."

Recognizing the importance of the job interview, you probably took the time to consider how you would present yourself for this important event. You might have spent hours selecting just the right outfit and practicing your answers to interview questions. On the day of your interview, you most likely made sure you left in plenty of time, allowed for traffic, and arrived early so as to make a good impression. You probably were careful to present yourself in the best possible manner during your job interview.

Some people have two distinct images: their *interview image* and their *employed image*. The person who was hired is the person who was at the interview. To change now would be unfair. Are you willing to put forth the same amount of effort you did for the interview day after day once you have the job? Hopefully, you will reinforce your employer's decision to hire you by being the kind of person your employer thought you were when you were hired.

There are potentially hundreds of applicants applying for any one position. A tremendous amount of time, labor, and money goes into the process of reviewing resumes, interviewing candidates, and checking references. Therefore, making the decision to hire someone is not taken lightly. Hiring the wrong person can have huge ramifications; if you fail to work out, it is a costly mistake and the process will need to begin all over again.

The manner in which you conduct yourself during your interview should be a true example of the kind of person you will be on the job day in and day out. If you act phony during the interview in order to get a job, you will not live up to the expectations of your employer. Try to go to work every day with the same kind of energy you had in the interview.

Evaluate and carefully plan for this new role you have assumed, and then do whatever is necessary to reinforce it every single day.

You might have a few doubts and fears after you accept a position, wondering if the job will be everything you hope it to be. Your employer has fears, too. One of your employer's greatest fears is that he or she made a mistake in hiring you.

Your employer has made an enormous commitment to you by hiring you. A tremendous amount of time and money goes into the hiring and training process. Once you have been selected, other well-qualified prospects have been told they didn't make the cut. If you end up working out well, the person who hired you has succeeded and will be given credit for his or her hiring ability. If you don't work out, it will reflect poorly on the person who hired you.

Your employer believes in you and assumes you are everything you appeared to be in the interview. Be the kind of person your employer will value. Validate the decision this company made to hire you every single day. The way you present yourself is just as important once you have a job as it was when you were interviewing for that job. And arriving on time is also critical. Continue to watch what you say and do. In fact, everything you do from this day forward on the job will either enhance or detract from your reputation and advancement opportunities.

SUMMARY

Remember:

- ✔ Be open to learning; you are embarking on one of your biggest and most important learning curves to date.

- ✔ Prepare for your new role; think about what kind of impression you want to make. Decide how you need to look and act.

- ✔ Be friendly. Introduce yourself to others, let your enthusiasm show, and don't forget to smile!

- ✔ Be the kind of employee you said you would be during your interview, and don't let your guard down or become too comfortable in your position.

- ✔ Your employer will have both spoken and unspoken expectations. Be aware of both.

- ✔ Know your employer's expectations and do whatever you can to meet and exceed those expectations.

- ✔ Play the part of a professional: act, look, and be at your best every single day.

Chapter 12

Communication Skills That Work at Getting and Keeping Work

HOW DO YOU SOUND TO OTHERS?

Have you ever heard yourself on an answering machine or listened to yourself on audiotape? What was your reaction? Most people are taken by surprise and react by saying, "That's not what I sound like!" We do sound differently to ourselves than we do to others.

The way you sound impacts your credibility and your image. It can determine how far you will go in an interview, whether or not you get a job offer, and your advancement opportunities. The following tips will help you to communicate clearly and sound pleasing to others:

Use appropriate grammar. You don't need to use big, impressive words to sound good to others. In fact, most people prefer simple language that is easy to understand. Avoid slang, jargon, and swearing, and if you feel it will help you, work on building your vocabulary and sentence structure.

Speak with a steady flow. When you speak, do your words flow? Or do you hem and haw, correct yourself, or undermine what you've said? The ability to think on your feet is an asset, so work on responding to questions and putting your thoughts together clearly.

Use good diction. If people frequently ask you to repeat yourself, you may not be communicating clearly. Make sure you enunciate and pronounce all words and sounds correctly, and avoid mumbling.

Eliminate excess verbiage. Using "ums" and "ahs" frequently in your conversation can be distracting to a listener. Try to speak clearly without using too many fillers.

Vary your inflection. If you vary your tone and inflection you will be more interesting to listen to. Avoid speaking in a monotone.

Add depth and confidence. You've probably heard people who "up-talk." They end every sentence "up," making their statements sound like questions. When this is done, people sound as though they are unsure about what they are saying. You are better off speaking in a slightly lower pitch than a higher one. Unless you are asking a question, don't end your sentences with "up-talk."

Watch your volume. There are situations when speaking loudly is an asset, for example, when you make a presentation to a large group or when you are in a noisy environment. Speaking too loudly in the wrong environment, however, will be disruptive to others and is not recommended. If you speak too softly, people may not pay attention to what you have to say or may discount your credibility.

Express warmth. Pause before you answer a telephone call. Take a deep breath if necessary, so that you sound welcoming to the caller. Greet a stranger on the phone as you would a call from a friend.

Be aware of the emotional quality of your voice. You don't want to sound aggravated, stressed, or in a hurry when you are on the phone. Avoid speaking too quickly or too slowly, and too loudly or too softly.

THE TELEPHONE: AN IMPORTANT BUSINESS TOOL

The telephone is a viable business tool, and using it effectively is essential to your success in finding a job and in your ability to get things done once you are working. There is more to using the telephone than picking it up to answer or dial out. When you interact with someone face to face, what you say is supported by your facial expressions and body language, which help clarify, support, and add interest to your words. On the telephone, the only way to enhance your words is by sounding animated and interesting. You can achieve this through your tone and inflection. Think about the broadcasters you hear on the radio. Although you can't see the person you are listening to, you can tell whether someone is actively involved or passionate about what they are saying. Imagine how boring it would be to listen to a broadcaster who spoke in a monotone for the entire broadcast. You can bet that the broadcasters who sound animated are acting that way.

Smile while you speak on the phone, so that you come across as friendly and enthusiastic. If you really want to add impact, try standing as you speak. This will add strength and energy to your voice. You may want to place a mirror by your phone as a reminder to express yourself in an energetic and lively manner.

HOLD THAT 'HOLD' BUTTON

Do you like being placed on hold? Most people don't, and when on hold, seconds seem like minutes. Always ask permission anytime you want to place someone on hold. Don't ever assume it is all right unless you've asked and waited for a reply. If you must place someone on hold, never leave the caller for more than 30 seconds without coming back and asking permission to put them on hold longer.

I was doing a radio interview by telephone a number of years ago and the interview wasn't going very well. It was apparent that the person interviewing me hadn't done any preparation, and she was having a difficult time getting into the conversation. Apparently, she thought that I was the problem, and when she put me on hold, she didn't press the right hold button because I heard her tell her producer, "This woman is boring. Let's get rid of her."

I was dumbfounded. I've been called many things, but *boring* has never been one of them! The lesson: Be sure to press the hold button and be careful about what you say when you place someone on hold. Return quickly when you do, and always thank the person for holding. Leaving someone on hold too long is not a good idea and can make the person feel as though he or she has been forgotten.

Call waiting or a second phone line is convenient for those occasions in which you simply cannot miss a call, but most people use them for more than an urgent situation. If you are talking with someone and another call comes in and you put the first caller on hold, you are placing more importance on the new caller than the person with whom you are talking. Placing someone on hold is an inconvenience to that person and doesn't show respect for their time. When you ignore call waiting, you make the person you are talking to your top priority, which should be your objective.

ANSWERING AND PLACING CALLS

The manner in which you answer the phone is both a reflection on you and the company for which you work. Once you are employed, find out if your company suggests answering the phone in a particular way. If your company does not have a preferred greeting, you will need to decide how you will answer the phone. When the telephone rings, try to answer it by the third ring or have it go to voicemail. No one likes to wait for five or more rings before getting an answer.

When calls come directly to you, and you know they are either internal or from a personal acquaintance, you can answer more casually than when answering calls from someone with whom you have not developed a working relationship. State your name when answering the phone. For internal calls, stating your first name is usually sufficient, but when answering calls that come directly to you from customers or others outside the company, you should use your first and last name.

For internal or personal callers, "This is John" or "John Johnson speaking" will suffice, but it doesn't hurt to add a touch of friendliness by saying, "Hello, this is John." However, when answering calls from outside callers, it is better to say, "Good morning, ABC Company, this is Anne Smith."

It is important to identify yourself when making an outbound call, too. Unless you know the person you are calling quite well, use both your first and last name along with your company name. "Hi Jan, this is Meg Tate with Arthur Investments calling."

When a receptionist or assistant answers a call, always identify yourself to that person. "Good morning, this is Meg Tate with Arthur Investments calling. Is Marc Jones available?"

Keep in mind that most people are inundated with phone calls every day. When you call someone, you are interrupting him or her and calling at your convenience, not necessarily a convenient time for that person. Make sure the person is able to talk before jumping into the conversation. And, no matter how well you think you know someone, never assume that person will recognize your voice; always state your name at the beginning of a conversation.

Chances are you won't always reach the person you are calling and you may find yourself in rounds of telephone tag with many people. You may find that you will be most successful in reaching people if you call first thing in the morning or late in the day. If you want to reach someone, it is your responsibility to continue to call until you do.

VOICEMAIL

You can accomplish quite a bit through voicemail, often without ever talking directly with someone. Learn to use voicemail to set lunch dates, meetings, and appointments, and to get answers to your questions.

When leaving a voicemail message for someone, keep in mind that your message is one of many the person you are calling will be receiving that day. Make your message brief and to the point. It is most helpful to write out the main points you want to cover so that you don't waste your time trying to decide what to say as you are recording. It is a good idea to leave your telephone number both at the beginning and end of a message. This way you can he sure the person has the number and it enables the receiver to ensure that he or she has written it correctly. When you leave your name and number, speak s-l-o-w-l-y. I can't tell you the number of times I have had difficulty writing down a number that has been left on my voicemail because the person said it too quickly. Try writing it as you say it and you will enable the person on the other end to do the same.

If you are struggling to reach someone, try to set a specific time for the two of you to talk. Leave a few options of times you will be available. If you have left several messages and have not received a return call, you need to evaluate the situation. If you've left several messages and attempted to reach someone and are getting no response, you should realize that the lack of a response is a response. The silence is telling you that the person is not interested. You may want to leave one final message, stating that it is the last time you will call for awhile. Be pleasant and leave the door open to future connections. It's important to know when to walk away. Many people update and change their voicemail daily. If you choose to do this, be sure you remember to change it each day. I've called people whose voicemail messages are weeks old. Hearing "I'll be out of the office until March 30" when it is April 15 does not send the right message to the caller.

Listen to your message before you use it to make sure you are pleased with the way it sounds. Try to sound upbeat and avoid a monotone delivery. If you say you will get back to the caller as soon as possible, be sure you do as you say and return calls promptly. When you fail to return a call, you are telling that person (by your silence), "I don't care about you," or "You're not important enough for me to call."

WORDS SEND A MESSAGE

The words you use when speaking are important in all business communication and especially important over the phone. Avoid slang, as it sounds too casual and youthful. Answering the phone by saying, "Yo" or "Hey" is too informal for the workplace, so is telling someone to "Hang on," instead of asking that person to please hold for a moment. Rather than saying, "How ya doin'?" say "How are you doing?" Always end a conversation by thanking the person for their time, and saying good-bye. Avoid phrases such as "Ba-bye" or "Talk to ya later."

If you answer a call for a coworker who is unavailable, there is no need to give a detailed description as to why the person can't come to the phone. Don't announce someone is in the restroom or taking a break. Simply state that the person is unavailable or has stepped away from his or her workspace for a moment.

SPEAKING ON SPEAKERPHONES

No one likes to have a phone on their ear or shoulder all day, which is why headsets and speakerphones are nice alternatives. The only danger with speakerphone is that when you use it, anyone and everyone within hearing distance of you can hear your conversation. Therefore, if you are listening to your messages on a speakerphone, be aware of other people overhearing what is being said.

Some people prefer to answer calls by pressing the speakerphone button, but it is better to answer the phone directly and ask permission to put the person on the speakerphone before doing so. No one likes to be placed on a speakerphone unknowingly and some people find it offensive, feeling as though you are too busy to take the time to pick up the phone to talk with them. The impression is that you may be doing other things as you are talking on the phone. Beware: The sound of hitting keys on your computer is amplified through the speakerphone, as are opening drawers and shuffling through paper.

It may be necessary to use a speakerphone when bringing together several people, but the same protocol applies. Begin the conversation through the mouthpiece and then ask each person to be included in the conversation for permission to turn on the speakerphone.

You also need to inform the person on the other end of the phone that this is a group call. Identify the people in the room and allow each person to say hello after being introduced. Then begin the conversation. It can be tricky to have a conference call this way, but it can be very effective if done properly. If you are one of many in a room, always announce your name before speaking so the person receiving the call knows who is speaking.

The following tips will help you use the phone more effectively.

Telephone Do's:

- Establish a professional way to answer your phone.
- Identify yourself with your first and last names and company name.
- Smile when you talk on the phone.
- State the purpose for your call at the beginning of the conversation.
- Keep your conversations brief and to the point.
- Pay full attention to the person on the phone.
- Ask permission to place someone on hold and thank that person for holding.
- Return all calls within one business day.
- Change your voicemail message daily or as needed.
- Answer your phone by the third ring.
- Speak courteously to everyone when calling a business, including the receptionist.

Telephone Don'ts:

- Take calls when you are with someone else.
- Eat, smoke, or chew gum while on the phone.

- Place someone on hold for more than 30 seconds.

- Say you will return a call if you won't.

- Engage in idle chitchat.

- Use the speakerphone without asking permission of the person with whom you are speaking.

- Type on your computer or rustle through papers while talking to someone.

- Use slang or profanity.

- Forget to update your voicemail message.

- Talk with someone else while on the phone.

- Yawn, sigh, or breathe too loudly.

PAGERS AND CELLULAR PHONES

It is a great convenience to be able to reach anyone, anytime, anywhere. It can also be intrusive and inconvenient. The ability to retreat and get away from everything (including the office) is becoming more and more difficult.

There are certain places and occasions in which you should turn your phone and pagers *off*. Anytime you are a part of an audience, whether at a movie, play or concert, listening to a speaker, in a meeting, or at a wedding or funeral, a ringing, beeping, or vibrating sound will be a distraction and an interruption. There is nothing as embarrassing as having all eyes on you as you struggle to answer or turn off your phone or pager. The simplest solution is to get into the habit of turning your phone or pager off when an incoming call would be inappropriate.

If there is some urgent or pressing reason you simply cannot wait until a break or intermission to check messages, then leave the room to turn on your phone and check. Unless putting your phone on silent really keeps it silent (and many do not), your phone should be turned off. Let it interrupt *you*, but there is no reason it needs to disturb everyone else.

When you are out for a meal, the same rule applies. If you take a call and ignore the person you are with, leaving him or her with nothing to do, the implied message is that the caller is more important than the person you are with.

If someone needs to reach you, they will reach you. Most calls can wait an hour or so. Be respectful and courteous of others and focus on the people you are with by turning your pager or phone off.

Another annoyance occurs when people have conversations on cellular phones that can be heard by everyone around them. Be discreet as to where you have your personal conversations and what you talk about. Most people don't want or need to know about the intimate details of your life, which are often discussed on the phone.

I was in a restroom and heard a woman engaged in a conversation on her phone. Toilets were flushing, people were coming and going, and she was in a stall having an intimate conversation. I couldn't believe it! A restroom is one of the most inappropriate places to talk on the phone.

E-MAIL ETIQUETTE

The Internet and e-mail have changed the way we do business. Efficient and effective, e-mail allows us to reach people and conduct business much faster than regular mail. Many people prefer to use e-mail to communicate instead of the telephone.

I received a question for my column from a reader who wondered how formally e-mail must be written. The reader assumed that e-mail was designed for efficiency and ease and didn't worry much about sending formal or structured e-mail. He didn't usually start with a "Dear John" or end with "Sincerely yours." Instead, he would cut and paste bits of information into his e-mail and send it without checking for spelling and grammar errors. It wasn't until one of his friends told him he was offended by his casual e-mail style, suggesting he write in a more formal tone, that he questioned the proper format of his e-mail.

I opened the topic up to all of my readers and asked their opinions on the subject. My readers were divided on this issue. Half felt as my writer did, that e-mail was meant to be fast and convenient, and that there was no need to worry about format or structure.

The other half felt that e-mail was the same as any type of business correspondence and that all letters should be written in a business format with correct spelling and punctuation.

I concluded that, at the risk of offending someone, you should never assume it is fine to be too casual in your correspondence. Begin all e-mail correspondence as you would any other type of correspondence. As you build a relationship with a person, take note of the manner in which he or she communicates with you and follow his or her lead. This is the safest way to ensure you won't offend anyone. However, even if someone sends you an e-mail with many mistakes, it doesn't mean you should do the same. Remember, e-mail can be saved, printed, and distributed. Before you press the 'send' button, be sure that what you are sending reflects positively on you and your company

Some of the e-mail slang and abbreviations you may use with friends may not be viewed favorably in the business world. Smiley faces have become one way to add some feeling to an e-mail, but they shouldn't be included in any business e-mail you send unless someone has sent you a smiley face first and you want to reciprocate.

Keep in mind that people are inundated with e-mail messages. E-mail is fast and easy, therefore readers are looking for fast and easy ways to delete messages and get through their mail.

You will maximize your e-mail efficiency if you:

- Write an effective, attention-grabbing subject line.

- State the purpose of your e-mail up front.

- Keep it short (most people won't scroll all the way down to read an entire e-mail).

- Write in a 10- or 12-point size.

- Do not write in all CAPS; it is the equivalent of SHOUTING at someone.

- Use spell check and proofread before sending.

- Use professional greetings and salutations.

- Include your name and contact information in your signature block.

- Check your e-mail frequently and respond quickly.

- Do not forward jokes, poems, or special promotions unless requested.

- Send important documents by regular mail, too.

- Use a professional, businesslike tone.

SURFING THE INTERNET

You will, undoubtedly, have access to the Internet through your computer at work. While this computer and the Internet are provided to you for business use, it is not your private computer to use as you wish. Many companies allow their employees to use the computer for personal use as well, and some provide laptops to be taken home.

Keep in mind that computer technology is very sophisticated. Your company has the right to, and likely will, monitor your Internet and e-mail use. Although most people use the Internet and their computers wisely, others take advantage and spend valuable work time surfing the Net. If you choose to do this, it is just a matter of time before someone catches on to you. Chances are either your work will suffer or you will. Use the Internet wisely and don't take advantage of having it at your fingertips.

MANAGING MEETINGS

Whether you are looking for work or already working, you will be required to attend meetings. As you take on more responsibility, the number of meetings you must attend may increase. Some people feel that too many meetings are a waste of time. If you are responsible for holding a meeting, be sensitive to the fact that you are taking people away from other important things they could be doing.

Meetings are most effective when they are brief and to the point. An agenda is always recommended, along with a specific starting and ending time. Where you sit will impact your involvement. The most powerful place to sit is at the head of the table facing the door, which allows you to see who is coming and going. The head of the table is usually reserved for the meeting leader. The middle of the table is considered one of the best places to sit, and sitting next to the leader is also a great place to be.

Even more important than where you sit is how you act and react during a meeting. Meetings are most effective when everyone participates fully. Give your full attention to the speaker and avoid side conversations with others. When asked to participate, get involved. When you speak, speak clearly, loudly, and confidently, and make sure you appear interested and involved.

Tips for Effective Meetings

- Arrive on time.

- Greet everyone.

- Have writing implements with you.

- Bring your calendar (in the event future meetings are planned).

- Sit upright.

- Wait to speak until others have finished.

- Keep your comments brief.

- Avoid straying away from the subject being discussed.

- Avoid making negative facial expressions or sounds (i.e., rolling the eyes, sighing, etc.).

- Avoid yawning.

- Turn your phone pager and all alarms off.

- Come prepared.

- Stay focused; avoid any and all distractions.

SUMMARY

Remember:

✔ Although you can't be seen when on the telephone, your attitude and personality come through. Keep a mirror by your phone to remind you that through your voice, you can be "seen."

✔ Pay attention to the way you sound to others. Pause before you answer the phone or place a call so that you come across as friendly and in control.

✔ The telephone is one of the best business tools you have. Use it wisely, and remember, a phone call to someone is an interruption to that person's schedule. Always have a purpose for your call and keep your conversations short and to the point.

✔ Make it a practice to return all calls within one business day.

✔ Update your outgoing voicemail message frequently, and when leaving messages for others, keep them brief. Always include your name and telephone number at the beginning and end of any message you leave.

✔ Limit your use of your personal, cellular phone in public and watch your conversation; you never know who may be listening.

✔ Arrive at all meetings on time, greet everyone you see, and participate fully.

Chapter 13

Habits of Successful People

IT TAKES MORE THAN SKILLS AND KNOWLEDGE TO BE SUCCESSFUL

Imagine you start out at a job the same time as someone else. Although you both have similar levels of knowledge and expertise, over the years one of you will achieve a greater level of success than the other. What do you think will determine who will be the one to excel?

If you've ever wondered what it takes to succeed, I can tell you there are no secrets to success. Some people excel by defying the odds, but most successful people have many qualities in common that make them successful.

One of the best-selling business books of all time is Stephen Covey's *Seven Habits of Highly Effective People* (Fireside, 1990). Businesses encourage employees to read books like Covey's and send employees to seminars with the intent of helping them embrace change and develop new habits in order to be more effective workers.

WHAT IS A HABIT?

So what exactly is a habit? *Funk and Wagnalls New International Dictionary of the English Language* defines a habit as: "A tendency toward an action or condition, which by repetition has become spontaneous."

Jami, one of my closest friends, is in the habit of exercising. I am in awe of her commitment to do some form of exercise every single day. I, too, value exercise and I try to exercise often, but that may be my problem because trying isn't the same as *doing*. Exercising daily is challenging for me because my schedule changes daily. I've found it difficult to make exercise a habit. Jami does some form of exercise every day. She will go out for a run in almost any kind of weather and even exercises when she isn't feeling well. I've asked her how she motivates herself. Her reply: "Exercising for me is like brushing my teeth, it's a habit. If I miss a day, I don't feel right. I don't even have to think about doing it, it's just something I do automatically."

We all have habits, both good and bad. As you become part of a work environment and evolve in your career, your habits will impact your success. You are likely to be presented with more opportunities throughout your career if you are able to develop good habits, especially the most practiced habits of successful people.

GENERATE ENTHUSIASM

When I was in college I had a friend named Lisa. She was an only child, but she had many friends who were like family to her. I used to tease her because, whenever I was with her, we always ran into people she knew and she claimed each person was "like a brother or sister." Lisa greeted everyone she met enthusiastically. Whenever I would call her, she would shriek with enthusiasm as she'd say, "Hi, Sue! How are you doing?" She was always excited to see or hear from anyone and, as a result, people loved being around her.

Over the years I evaluated what made Lisa so popular and well liked, and I attributed it to her enthusiasm. Although I considered myself a cheerful person, I wondered if I could increase my enthusiasm. I made an effort to make people feel important by being excited when I would see them or hear from them. A friend once told me that I always sounded tired and irritated when I answered my phone, so I decided to answer with more enthusiasm. I am sure that my improved attitude encouraged my friends to call me more often, and I know it has helped me throughout my career.

Think about a memorable concert or sporting event you've attended. What is the difference between attending these events live and watching them on television? Sitting in front of the television often provides a better view, but sitting in the stands surrounded by other fans often makes the event more exciting. A big part of that enjoyment comes from the energy and enthusiasm of the crowd. Enthusiasm is contagious.

Think about the many teachers you've had over the years and you'll probably find that the ones who stand out were enthusiastic about teaching. Think about the people with whom you enjoy associating. There are people who light up a room when they enter it. You actually feel better just being around them. And then there are people who light up a room when they *leave* it. They are dull, boring, and depressing. Think about *you*; what does *your* presence generate—an increase in energy or a loss of it? Do you light a room? If not, why not? Think about it.

IMPROVE YOUR ATTITUDE

After a long day, I was ready to settle down in my hotel room, eat dinner, and get a good night's sleep before my seminar the next day. Ordering and receiving room service is something I do frequently when I travel and it is usually uneventful. But when Ruby, a room service worker, waltzed in and greeted me with her enthusiastic hello, welcoming me to Detroit, I was taken by surprise.

She offered her hand for a handshake and began chatting with me as though we'd known each other for years. I had requested a pot of hot water to help me nurse the cold I was hanging on to, but it wasn't put on the order. Ruby was quick to assure me the water would be delivered. She went to the concierge to get it because it would be faster than going to the kitchen. When Ruby returned, she was so excited to be able to serve me the hot water in a beautiful silver pitcher. Concerned that I might burn myself, she instructed me to use the napkin when holding the handle.

The fact that Ruby was called back to my room because my order came undercooked didn't faze her. In fact, she was delighted to see me again and told me to be sure to ask for her the next night of my stay. It made me feel good to know that she cared so much.

The next night when I placed my order, I requested Ruby. When she came to deliver my meal, it was like greeting an old friend. "How is your cold today?" she inquired. We chatted about the day, and before she left I told her how impressed I was with her and that I wanted to send her a copy of my book, *How to Gain the Professional Edge.* Tears welled up in her eyes as she hugged me and told me that I had made her day.

Typically, hugging a customer would be taboo, but with Ruby it felt natural. "I love people," she explained. "I get compliments all the time, and my boss told me to keep doing whatever I am doing because it's working. I love what I do and I am blessed with the gift of loving people."

I mailed her my book and received a thank you note from her along with a picture she had taken of herself, smiling and holding the book. That picture sits on a shelf in my office and every time I look at it, I smile.

Some people would say that Ruby's role as a server was insignificant—a low-level position in the hotel business. But think again. Without someone to serve food, how would a hotel take care of its guests? Every position is important, and Ruby had the sense to know that what she did mattered. She also knew that her customers mattered. She went beyond what was expected of her and everyone reaped the benefits. Customers and management were happier and she undoubtedly received bigger tips and positive feedback because of her exceptional attitude.

I meet many people in my travels, but few who touch me as Ruby did. Ruby truly is blessed with a gift and is an example of someone we all can learn from. Bless yourself with the gift of loving people.

STAND UP FOR YOURSELF

My daughter Stephanie worked as a nanny for a family. They were going on a vacation and asked her to drive them to the airport. She agreed to take them even though it meant waking up at 3:30 in the morning in order to pick them up at 4:00 A.M. When Stephanie told me her plans, not only was I concerned about her driving the 25 miles to and from the airport in the middle of the night, but because she was not yet 18, she could be fined if she was caught driving after midnight.

Stephanie didn't really want to have to take this family to the airport, but she didn't know how to decline and was afraid that if she did, the people would be mad at her. "So what if they are mad at you?" I asked her. "You should be mad at them for asking you to get up in the middle of the night to drive them to the airport. They can call a cab." I insisted she call and tell them she couldn't drive them, even giving her permission to blame it all on me. She was petrified of their reaction and begged me to let her drive them. I ended up making the call to tell them that Stephanie was unable to take them to the airport. I told them the reasons why. The woman was most understanding and hadn't even been aware of the curfew.

Why would Stephanie be more concerned about their needs than her own? Why was she afraid to stand up for herself? Perhaps her age and her desire to please others played a role in her reticence. However, no matter what your age or circumstance, if you feel uncomfortable with a request someone makes, you need to honor that feeling. If you do not like the way someone treats you, you need to let that person know. If you don't stand up for yourself, why should anyone else? Unless you stand up for yourself and establish boundaries, people will treat you however they want.

Dr. Phil McGraw, talk show host and best-selling author, says that we teach people how to treat us. How are you teaching others to treat you?

BE A TEAM PLAYER

No matter what job you hold, your performance is important and you add value to an organization. If you have ever been involved in sports, you probably learned a lot about the importance of being a part of a team and how to be a team player. The people you work with are part of a team. When you begin your new job, you will be the newest team member.

If you view yourself as part of a team, then you will realize that the work you do is significant and part of the whole. Don't isolate yourself. The job you do is essential but not the only important job to be done. Work with others and be willing to pitch in and help out even when the duty isn't in your job description. If you do, your team members will view you favorably. Think in terms of being a part of a team—a very good habit to have.

BE PROACTIVE

Imagine you have a job interview with a company you really want to work for. This is a dream job: a great starting salary, good benefits, room for growth, and plenty of flexibility. On the morning of the interview, you take extra time to prepare and leave early to make sure you arrive on time.

You are driving along and suddenly realize you have a flat tire. You pull over and are about to react to what has happened. How might you respond? What do you think a typical reaction might be?

I've used this scenario in my seminars many times, and based on the responses from my seminar participants, the first reaction most people say they would have is anger—that they would get mad. Upon discovering the flat tire you, too, might be angry and swear, yell, cry, pound on the steering wheel, or even get out of the car and kick the tire.

You may begin to experience feelings of despair and decide you are destined for failure and/or bad luck. You might even come to the conclusion that the job wasn't meant to be and give up.

These are common reactions, but will do nothing to help you in such a situation. Reacting by getting angry won't do anything to change the fact that you have an interview to get to and no transportation. So what choices do you have? You can refuse to react by becoming proactive instead. You can say to yourself, "So what, *now what?*" "What am I going to do about the fact that my tire is flat and I need to arrive in 15 minutes or risk missing the interview?" When you are proactive, not reactive, you focus on what you *can* do and think of solutions and ways to gain control of the situation.

So what are your options? You could make a telephone call (for a cab, a tow truck, or to the person you will be meeting with) and explain what has happened. You can change the tire. You can start walking. One participant in a seminar said she would call ahead to explain what happened *and* have doughnuts and coffee sent to the office in the meantime! Now that's proactive! You can take control of what happens rather than let it take control of you.

BRING OUT THE BEST IN OTHERS

Can you remember the last compliment you received? When was the last time you paid someone else a compliment? Are you free with praise for others? Some people hold back positive comments because they are afraid it will boost someone's ego or that complimenting others will somehow take away something from themselves. Although some people become embarrassed when receiving a compliment, most people welcome a flattering remark.

Your comfort level may reflect what you are used to hearing. If you grew up in an environment in which you received positive remarks about yourself, you may be comfortable giving and receiving compliments. If praise was withheld, you may find that you, too, hold back and aren't comfortable complimenting others.

People crave appreciation and will work harder to please you when they know their efforts will be appreciated. Successful managers know that praising an employee can be equally important as, if not more important than, financial rewards. Bob Nelson, a well-known speaker and author of the book *1001 Ways to Reward Employees* (Workman Publishing, 1994), has made a business out of helping managers find ways to reward employees. Showing appreciation and complimenting others is not something that comes easily or naturally to many people.

Have you ever complimented someone only to have the person negate what you've said? I've noticed that many people do this. I teach a class on presentation skills, and because people are so uncomfortable speaking before a group, I've found that it is difficult for many of them to accept any positive remarks about their presentations. In fact, I've had people challenge me when I've given positive feedback by trying to convince me that their presentation was terrible and refusing to accept my observations. If you are given a compliment, the best thing to do is to simply say, "thank you." Don't challenge someone's position or try to convince him or her that you don't deserve the compliment.

Look for the good in people and be free and sincere with your comments and compliments. People crave positive reinforcement. You lose nothing by giving positive feedback to others. In fact, you will gain. Every time I am able to make someone else look or feel good, I look and feel good, too.

In his book, *How to Win Friends and Influence People* (Pocket Books, 1994), Dale Carnegie says that giving honest, sincere appreciation is the key to dealing with people and that people will cherish your words and treasure them long after you have forgotten them. When you pay someone a compliment, be specific. Rather than telling someone, "I liked your presentation," find something specific about the presentation you liked. For example, say, "1 liked it when you opened up and shared your personal experiences in your presentation. I feel as though I understand you and the importance of your message better now."

Try to avoid commenting too much on appearance as your intentions could be misunderstood. But do look for opportunities to bring out the best in others.

BE ON TIME

Punctuality is one habit that many people find challenging. Rarely does someone plan on arriving late, but many people are consistently late for work, appointments, meetings, and other engagements. We've already discussed the importance of arriving on time and even a few minutes early for an interview and for work, but being on time is equally as important once you have a job.

You may arrive late without hearing a comment from anyone, but believe me, it is noticed. Of course there is the occasional tardiness that is acceptable and understandable due to bad weather, heavy traffic, emergencies, or illness. However, when you are habitually late, you begin to draw attention to yourself, and your capability in other areas may be questioned. People may perceive you as negligent, disrespectful, disorganized, or incompetent.

If it is important to you to be on time, you will be on time. Therefore, when you are late for work or for an appointment, you are making the statement that you don't value your job or the time of the person you are scheduled to meet. Get into the habit of arriving a few minutes early. Then if you do run into a problem, you will have the necessary extra time to work through it and still arrive on time.

KEEP YOUR WORD

I've run into an old friend of mine every now and then and every time we see each other she says, "We have to get together soon. I'll call you." But she never does. She's not the only one who makes empty promises. Many of us tell others what we believe they want to hear. But think before you speak. If people learn that they can't depend on what you say, they're likely to assume they can't count on *you*.

If you say you will have something done by the end of the day, have it done by the end of the day. If you say you will call someone back by 5:00 P.M., call that person back by 5:00 P.M. If you say you will do something, do it. If you miss too many deadlines, break too many promises, and fail to keep your word, people will quickly learn they can't depend on you and, unfortunately, it will be true.

RESPECT OTHERS

The way you treat people reflects your values and feelings about them. In the workplace, manners do matter. Displaying good manners shows you respect people and common courtesies help put others at ease.

Little things make a major difference. Saying "please" when requesting something is less demanding than a command. Saying "thank you" when someone does something for you shows your appreciation.

Certain behaviors are considered crude and need to be avoided in the workplace. Chewing and snapping gum, burping and belching, or passing gas any other way, and talking loudly or about inappropriate matters need to be avoided. Any action that has the potential to offend someone should also be avoided, including telling offensive jokes, making inappropriate comments, gossiping, or swearing. Your best insurance against offending someone is to act with caution and be respectful of others at all times, regardless of their position.

BE CONSIDERATE

Consideration of others is not only common sense, it's also common courtesy. When you are working with others, even the smallest gesture of kindness will go a long way, such as:

- If you use the last piece of paper in the copier or fax machine, refill the paper bin.

- If you are running to the coffee shop, offer to get something for someone else.

- If you finish the coffee in the coffee pot, make another pot of coffee.

- If someone is on the phone or talking with someone, don't interrupt.

- If you are about to begin a conversation with a coworker near others who are diligently working, go somewhere else so you won't disturb anyone.

- If you need a stapler, pencil, or paper clip, ask before you take it from someone's desk.

- If you borrow something from someone, return it.

- If you make a mess, clean it up.

- If you smoke, smoke in designated areas.

PROMOTE YOURSELF

Self-promotion can be defined in many ways. There are people who manage to toot their own horn and delight in talking about their accomplishments. However, many people feel uncomfortable talking or boasting about what they have done.

Self-promotion is more than tooting your own horn. In fact, someone who is effective at promoting him- or herself often does it in a way that isn't obvious to others and so it doesn't seem self-serving.

Self-promoters are confident people who present themselves in the best possible manner at all times. You, too, can promote yourself by doing the following:

Emphasize the positive. Do you build yourself up and focus on your strengths or do you tear yourself down and dwell on your shortcomings? Watch the words you use when talking about yourself; if you demean or question yourself, you cause others to do the same because you know you best.

Get involved. Do you make things happen or wait for opportunities to come to you? Are you willing to take on a challenge or do you prefer the status quo? Do you volunteer to help out even when you may not benefit directly or do you avoid involvement if there's nothing in it for you? Don't sit back, hoping for opportunity; go after what you want. Get involved.

Distinguish yourself. If you want to set yourself apart from others, you must know what makes you uniquely you. The qualities and characteristics you overlook as insignificant may hold the key to what differentiates you from others.

Get into the forefront. Put your name "out there." Reach out to others. Be the first to say hello, the first to initiate a conversation. Get connected, and then stay connected through brief e-mails, a personal note, or a quick phone call every now and then.

Stand out. If you want to get noticed, you have to do more than blend in; you need to stand out. Don't go around telling people how great you are; let them *see* for themselves. Do something worth noticing.

SUMMARY

Remember:

- ✔ It takes more than skill and knowledge to do a job well. Eighty-five percent of the reason you will land a job, keep a job, or move ahead in a job will be based on your leadership skills, your ability to interact and get along with others, and your attitude.

- ✔ Be enthusiastic. Be the type of person who lights up a room with your presence. Approach your work and everything you do with enthusiasm. You will have more fun and, ultimately, be more effective.

- ✔ Improve your attitude. Bless yourself with the gift of loving people.

- ✔ Be a team player. Learn to work with others and be willing to do more than is expected. When a team succeeds, everyone is a winner.

- ✔ Be proactive. The next time you face a problem, don't dwell on it. Just ask yourself what you can do about what's happened. Take control of a situation by saying, "So what, *now what?*" before you react or decide what to do.

- ✔ Bring out the best in others. Look for the good in others, and be the first to comment on a job well done. You will feel good and make others feel good as well. When you receive a compliment, accept it by saying "thank you." Don't ever contradict someone's positive opinion of you.

✔ Respect others. How you treat others is a reflection of how you value them. Many of the issues relating to gender, diversity, and harassment at work could be eliminated if everyone lived with respect for others. Show your respect for others by treating everyone courteously and respectfully.

✔ Be considerate of others. Consideration of others is not only common sense, it's also common courtesy. Be sensitive to the needs of those with whom you work. Even the smallest gesture of kindness goes a long way, and it may be the one thing that makes someone's day.

✔ Promote yourself. If you want to get noticed, you have to do more than blend in; you need to stand out. Don't sit back, hoping for opportunity; go after what you want.

Chapter 14

Getting Along with Others

ALL ABOUT COMMITMENT AND RELATIONSHIPS

Think about the variety of relationships you have. Which ones are most important to you and why? You probably have a number of casual relationships, people who are in your life that you consider friends, even though you don't spend much time with them. You likely have other, closer relationships with people who are more involved in your day-to-day existence. Perhaps you've seen some of your relationships come and go. What is the reason some outlasted others? Chances are it has to do with the quality and importance of the relationship and your commitment to it.

When you accept a job offer, you enter into a new relationship, and you have made a commitment to that relationship. Commitment levels vary from person to person. Have you thought about the kind of commitment you are willing to make once you accept an offer? It may help to view your new job as you would a new relationship. The following questions will help you determine your level of commitment:

Once you've accepted a job, how long do you plan on staying with the company?

If you plan on working there for a year or more, chances are you will take the job more seriously than if you view it as a short-term position or a launching pad for something better. Max Messmer, author of *Job Hunting for Dummies* (Hungry Minds, 1999), advises professionals to consider the long-term implications of frequent job moves. Companies look for a pattern of stability in new hires in order to reduce the risk of turnover.

Are you satisfied with your decision to work at this company?

Did you take the first offer that came along or compromise what you really wanted because you needed a job? If you are not satisfied at the onset of a job, you may never be happy working there. If you are truly unhappy, admit you made a mistake and leave before investing (and wasting) too much time.

Do you plan on continuing your job search (even though you are employed) so that you can keep your options open?

If so, you may never really take this job seriously. If you never end your search and continue to look for something better, you may not be able to give this job a fair chance.

If you become disillusioned and discover that this job isn't everything you had hoped it would be, will you leave?

It's almost certain that at some point you will become disillusioned with your job. If you choose to leave a job every time this happens, you may find yourself job-hopping more than you planned. Your reaction will depend upon your level of commitment to this job. Many problems can be overcome, but you have to be willing to stay around to work things out.

If you are concerned or upset about something, will you talk about it with the appropriate people or are you the type who will keep your feelings to yourself?

Your answer to this question probably has a lot to do with the way you were brought up and your comfort level in expressing yourself. As in any relationship, if you are upset about something but say nothing, you will accomplish nothing. It is important to address issues that arise and to be honest with yourself, your supervisor, and your coworkers.

Are you looking to do your job as it's stated in your job description or are you willing to do whatever it takes to get the job done?

A detailed job description will help you understand what is expected of you. However, there are other expectations your employer has of you that are implied rather than written or spoken. If you are willing to do more than what is expected, you will get more than you expect.

Relationships require time, effort, and hard work. You and your employer have entered into a partnership, and both partners must make contributions to the relationship for it to work out. Make sure you do your share of contributing.

THE LIKEABILITY FACTOR

One of the biggest sources of irritation for many people is learning to cope with a difficult person, which varies from someone who is simply annoying to someone who is bad-tempered. The last thing you need is to be viewed as stubborn or difficult. What you do need is to have a high likeability factor.

Typically, in addition to being effective in their jobs, successful people often are likeable as well. Not only can these people perform the necessary tasks of a job, but they also interact well with people.

How Likeable Are You?

- Do you like people?

- Are you interested in what others have to say?

- Do you look on the bright side of things?

- Do you smile often?

- Do other people smile often at you?

- Are you a good listener?
- Do people confide in you?
- Are you a cheerful person?
- Do you compliment others easily?
- Are you happy with yourself?

If you answered yes to most of the questions, it is probable that you are very likeable. Read on to understand why.

Do you like people?

If you like people, you will approach all people positively and have a natural enthusiasm around others. As a result, people will enjoy being around you and, ultimately, like you, too.

Are you interested in what others have to say?

If you are sincerely interested in others, you will make people feel valued and cared about. Asking questions and taking an interest in others makes them feel important. If you make people feel valued, they will value you.

Do you look on the bright side of things?

If you are optimistic and tend to look on the bright side of things, people will enjoy being in your presence. There is plenty of gloom and doom in the world. Most people want to be hopeful and hear the positive spin on things.

Do you smile often?

A smile tells others you are happy and friendly. Some people never smile, and as a result, they come across as hostile or uninterested.

Do other people smile often at you?

If people smile at you, you probably smile a lot yourself and are viewed as approachable and friendly.

Are you a good listener?

Do you listen when someone is talking rather than concentrate on what *you* want to say? Good listeners invite people to open up and show they care about what is being said.

Do people confide in you?

When people confide in you, it is an indication they are comfortable talking to you and that they trust you. Consider yourself fortunate; someone confiding in you is a compliment.

Are you a cheerful person?

Given a choice, most people prefer to associate with cheerful people. Being cheerful is easy and uncomplicated and makes everything more enjoyable.

Do you compliment others easily?

Everyone can use a nice compliment—people crave appreciation. If you bring out the best in others, you bring out the best in yourself. Make others look good and you will look good in return.

Are you happy with yourself?

If you like yourself, people will notice and want to be around you. You will also find it easier to be supportive and complimentary of others if you are comfortable with who you are.

IF YOU LIKE PEOPLE, PEOPLE WILL LIKE YOU

Jeanne has worked for my family for years. She started out helping my mother with housework when I was a teenager and eventually began helping me once I was married and had a job. She has worked for my family for over 25 years. She has stayed with my children when I've been out of town and has been willing to do almost anything to help me out.

Jeanne has worked for a number of other people over the years but hasn't stayed with all of them. One day, after I heard she quit working for someone I knew, I was concerned that she would be quitting me, too. Her response surprised me. She said, "Oh, you don't have to worry about me leaving. I like you too much, and I like working for you."

Jeanne wasn't just working for the money. She *liked* working for me. And you know what? I liked having her work for me, too. I still do. And I always thank her for her diligence, because I really do appreciate her.

Frequently people will come up to me after a seminar and ask me for feedback. They want me to assess how they are doing and how they come across. I rarely critique anyone without a specific objective, but I can tell anyone how to critique and evaluate him- or herself.

We all receive feedback from others every day, but sometimes we fail to notice. The feedback is evident by the way people respond to us. How do people respond to you?

Do you:

- Think most people are difficult to get along with?
- Distrust people?
- Believe people are insincere?
- Consider people to be self-centered?
- Feel as though nothing good ever comes your way?

If you answered yes to any of the preceding questions, it is possible you have negative expectations and, as a result, are likely to attract what you expect (negativity) rather than what you desire (good things). Focus on what you want, rather than on what you lack, and reread this chapter to help you understand what you need to do to attract more of what you want.

PUT THINGS INTO PERSPECTIVE

A number of years ago, I worked with a woman who viewed everything negatively. She had trouble getting along with people at work, was frequently disappointed in her friends, and had cut herself off from her family because she couldn't get along with any of them.

Negative people make life miserable for everyone, yet they rarely see themselves as the problem, often blaming others for their unhappiness. One negative person can change the tone of an entire group of people.

How refreshing it is to be around someone who is upbeat, energetic, and positive. You will draw people to you if you are a positive person, and you will push people away with negativity. It is possible to find some good in what appears to be even the bleakest situations.

Don, an acquaintance of mine, became a quadriplegic shortly after graduating from high school. He was out for a motorcycle ride, was hit by someone driving a car (who left the scene), and was thrown from his bike. His life changed forever.

When he learned that he would never walk again, Don began using drugs to numb the emotional pain. He really didn't care about living anymore. Fortunately, he received the help he needed to overcome his drug addiction and despair. He decided that he wanted to live. He learned to draw by holding a pencil in his mouth and began creating beautiful pictures and greeting cards.

Today, in addition to selling his artwork, Don speaks to children and teenagers, empowering them to stay away from drugs, and encouraging them to develop a "can-do" attitude. His presence and uplifting spirit are extremely powerful. I have had the good fortune of hearing Don speak on a number of occasions and can tell you that he is one of the most inspiring people I have ever met.

Positive people can be found everywhere. Sometimes they appear when you least expect it. A few years ago I flew into Chicago on a cold and snowy evening. I was tired and hungry as a result of a long day and somewhat irritated because my flight had been delayed.

Once I got into the cab, the driver, who was very talkative, introduced himself and tried to make conversation with me. I wasn't very receptive. I was tired and just wanted to be alone in my thoughts. But Felix persisted and was so pleasant that it was difficult for me to avoid engaging in a conversation with him. Suddenly I realized that talking with him might be just what I needed to make a shift in my attitude and that perhaps there was a reason 1 was in that particular cab with this driver.

I started to listen to Felix and asked him questions. He told me he had escaped from Cuba to the United States over 15 years ago and he had been desperate to leave his country. Felix lived in hiding for two months prior to his escape, which took place in the middle of a driving rainstorm. He made the trip on a homemade, one-person boat built out of old truck tires. He spent over a week on this boat on the ocean and came close to death, but was fortunate enough to be rescued and become a U.S. citizen. His love of this country, the family he has created, and the obstacles he has overcome inspired and moved me.

Felix had such a positive outlook on life and told me he believes that life is what we choose to make of it. Listening to his life story and talking with him was uplifting. My frustration over running behind schedule was put into perspective. I became a different (and better) person as a result of that cab ride. I was able to let go of my previous frustration because I connected with another human being. I had been willing to distance myself from him and retreat into my own little world. Instead, I met someone who made me feel good about being alive and living in the United States, which is something I must admit I fail to think about some days.

Perhaps you've heard the saying, "When the teacher is ready, the student will appear." We are all students (of life) and everyone we meet has the ability to teach us something. Some of the most difficult people and challenging situations provide us with the most insight about ourselves and educate us about life.

You are young and new to the workplace. You are not yet burned out from years of work. You can bring a sense of exhilaration and anticipation to this new job that many of your older coworkers have lost over the years. If you are energized, don't stifle yourself; infuse everyone around you with that energy. You can be an inspiration for others; you can be a breath of fresh air for your department or entire company. Be that person and you will see what a difference you can make.

LEARN FROM DIFFICULT PEOPLE AND SITUATIONS

In her junior year of high school, my daughter Stephanie had a chemistry teacher who was in his final year of teaching. It was obvious he was counting the days until he could retire. He no longer cared about his students or about doing a good job. After seeing other students humiliated for asking questions in class, she stopped participating in discussions. Some days she would purposely miss his class in order to avoid him. Although many parents and students complained about him and his unusual tactics, nothing could be done. He would soon be gone, but not soon enough.

Stephanie was upset and angry. She didn't do well in his class and blamed him for ruining her grade point average. At times, she would cry just thinking about her grades. She couldn't find any reason for this to have happened, but I had a feeling that, if nothing else, this would teach her an important lesson about life.

If Stephanie failed chemistry, only she would suffer. Although there was nothing that could be done about this teacher, I told my daughter that she *could* learn something from him and become a better person as a result.

You will encounter many difficult people throughout your life. Some people know no other way to get attention, others manipulate people in order to maintain control, and some people simply never learned the art of getting along with others. You can't avoid difficult people, but you can avoid becoming like them and giving up who you are in their presence.

I am more compassionate toward people with disabilities as a result of knowing Don. I have a greater appreciation for the opportunities that are available in this country as the result of meeting Felix. I am even more appreciative of the many great teachers my children have had after experiencing what a poor teacher is like. Everyone we meet has the potential to influence us, and we have the potential to influence everyone we encounter. Think about what kind of influence you want to have on others and how you want your relationships with others to be. If you want to get along well with others, it will take effort on your part. It's your choice and a decision only you can make.

SOLVE AND RESOLVE PROBLEMS

It is inevitable: You will be faced with challenges at different times throughout your career and life. How you handle stress and the manner in which you deal with conflict will make a difference in the way you are perceived, and it will impact your overall effectiveness on the job.

Whether at work with managers, coworkers, or customers, or at home with family and friends, we all deal with conflict at one time or another. Although many people will do almost anything to avoid conflict, it is impossible because conflict is an inevitable part of human relationships. Conflict can be a vehicle, rather than a roadblock, to help you reach a new level of understanding. Many disputes can actually work for, rather than *against,* you. When you attempt to truly resolve a conflict rather than resist it, you have taken the first step toward using conflict constructively.

- Do you watch television?
- Do you read suspense novels?
- Do you enjoy watching movies?
- Do you tune in to the evening news?
- Do you read a newspaper?
- Do you enjoy sporting events
- Do you watch people debate?

If you answered yes to any of these questions, then perhaps you do embrace conflict because all of these activities involve some type of conflict. Most television shows, novels, and movies are filled with drama, suspense, action, and adventure. Many television and radio programs thrive and focus on conflict and controversy. Perhaps we are interested in viewing conflict because the conflict belongs to someone else. It is different when we are a part of the conflict.

Problems are inevitable. Don't become too anxious when someone complains to you. Be appreciative. Anytime anyone gives you feedback, whether good or bad, you can learn something of value.

The following tips will help you handle conflict and maintain good relationships with others:

- **Address issues while they are small.** Don't allow little irritations to fester and grow or they will escalate into bigger problems. Know what is worth addressing and what things should be overlooked. When you approach someone, be direct, but not defensive; be assertive, but not accusatory; and be specific, but not nitpicky.

- **Control your emotions.** Know your triggers and find a way to manage them. If you are easily frustrated or get mad over little things, work on calming yourself. When you feel yourself ready to blow up or lash out at someone, do what you can to get into the frame of mind to calmly deal with the conflict. Taking deep breaths or stepping away for a moment is sometimes all it takes.

- **Be open to others.** Be the type of person others are comfortable talking to and venting with, if necessary. If someone has a problem with you but cannot approach you, he or she is more likely to repress the anger. Worse yet, he or she might gossip about you to other people. Encourage honesty and feedback from others and accept it graciously.

- **Be a good listener.** Studies have shown that most of us are poor listeners and that we retain only 25 percent of what we hear. This indicates that we miss 75 percent of what is communicated to us! Listen to what others are saying, and remember, you have two ears and one mouth. Use them proportionately.

- **Be empathetic.** Take the time to understand another person's point of view. Try to put yourself in his or her shoes. Even if you don't agree with someone, you can make an effort to respect and understand his or her point of view.

- **Be direct.** If you have a problem with someone, take it directly to that person. Avoid complaining, gossiping, or talking with others about a problem that doesn't involve them.

- **Take ownership.** Rather than pointing fingers and placing blame on others, ask yourself what you may have done to contribute to the situation. When confronting someone, speak in terms of *I* rather than *you*. For example, say, "*I* feel as though we are all responsible for cleaning out the coffee pot," instead of, "*You* never do anything around here. When was the last time *you* cleaned out the coffee pot?"

- **Address problems immediately.** If you are upset about something, address it. Don't hold in your feelings or you may build resentment, and one day you may explode.

- **Set aside time to talk about a problem.** Don't barge into someone's office and start discussing an important issue when the mood strikes. Ask the person in advance for time to talk, and then find a quiet place where your conversation won't be interrupted.

- **Follow the appropriate chain of command.** It is important to honor the hierarchy within your organization, as you risk alienating others if you don't. If you have no luck and nothing changes once you've addressed the issue with the person you are having the problem with, then follow the appropriate channels.

- **Nurture relationships.** Regardless of title or rank, treat everyone equally and respectfully. Take time to get to know the people you work with and to build solid relationships. If you are struggling with someone, make an effort to get to know more about him or her. Ask for a lunch date or take a break together. Strong relationships can withstand most conflict.

YOUR SECOND FAMILY

You are likely to develop friendships with some of your coworkers. In fact, you may discover that the people at work become like a second family. You will see the members of this "family" day in and day out, much more than you see anyone else, be it a real family member or friend.

Every day you will find yourself greeting many different people. You'll see the receptionist; coworkers; people in the hall, on the elevator, at the coffee shop, and in the cafeteria. You will acknowledge many of these people quite frequently, but may find yourself at a loss for words after you say hello.

It can be awkward to sit next to someone in silence as you wait for a meeting to begin. Your ability to carry on a conversation will be an asset and is crucial to your success. If you are sincerely interested in other people, you are already on your way to becoming a good conversationalist; you don't need to talk a lot to be interesting. People love to talk about themselves, and if you have a sincere interest in others, they will love being around you. All you need to do is ask the right questions, listen, and respond.

To generate a conversation, you need to establish a common ground with someone. You want to give people a reason to talk with you. This can be difficult to do when you have just met someone, but by asking the right questions and picking a safe topic you should be able to lead and develop a conversation with almost anyone. The difference is in knowing how to ask a question that leads to a conversation (also known as a *conversation starter*), or a question that leads nowhere or alienates the other person (*conversation stopper*).

CONVERSATION STARTERS

The following conversation starters are generally not controversial and are neutral topics that should enable you to establish rapport with anyone and carry on a conversation:

- the weather
- sports
- current events
- food/restaurants
- music
- movies
- books
- vacations/travel
- family
- work
- hobbies

Here's how a conversation might progress:

Eric: How long have you been working here?

Kim: I've been here for five years.

Eric: That's great! What department do you work in?

Kim: I'm in advertising.

Eric: So what school did you go to?

Kim: I went to the University of Minnesota

Notice that Eric didn't stop after one question, but continued to probe and appear interested. However, Eric would be better off asking questions that require more of a response. Notice how he finally gets Kim to talk more as the conversation progresses:

Eric: No kidding! My best friend is from Minnesota. He always tells me how cold the winters are. In fact, when I visited him it was something like 20 below zero! How did you deal with the weather?

Kim: Well, I'll tell you, it was a real shock to my system. I'm from the South, and we considered it a cold day when it was 50 degrees! I heard it was cold but had no idea how cold it could get. Where in Minnesota does your friend live?

In this conversation, Eric contributed more to the conversation by sharing some information and then turning the conversation back over to Kim. If Kim is astute, she should ask Eric questions about himself, too, which she finally did.

Asking open-ended questions will increase your chances of getting a *response,* rather than an *answer* from someone. For example, an open-ended question could be: "How did you get into this line of work?" The question requires a response. By asking open-ended questions, you increase your chance of carrying on a conversation with someone. In contrast, a closed question such as, "You work in the accounting department, don't you?" requires a simple yes or no answer and will not lead to a conversation very easily. As long as you are sincerely interested, your questions should lead into a naturally flowing conversation.

CONVERSATION STOPPERS

Conversation stoppers are questions or comments that fail to lead to further discussion. Refrain from asking personal questions or from appearing nosy or intrusive. Some topics are riskier than others. You are wise to stay away from asking questions or talking about:

- personal finances/money
- romance/relationships
- sex
- politics

- religion

- weight/diets

- divorce

- illness/death

- other people/gossip

- controversial subjects

- personal problems

For example, beginning a conversation with, "I feel lousy today—I think I am getting the flu," will push people away from you. No one wants to hear your complaints, and no one wants to catch what you've got. Your goal is to make others feel comfortable around you. Why bring up any subject that has the potential to create an awkward situation?

TALKING WITH SUPERVISORS, COWORKERS, AND CUSTOMERS

I was sitting in the beautiful lobby of an insurance company waiting to meet with someone. It was shortly after the noon hour and the lobby was busy with people coming and going. Two women stood in the middle of the lobby, and although I wasn't trying to eavesdrop, I couldn't help but overhear their conversation. Once I realized what they were talking about, I was shocked. Apparently, one of the women had some health problems and had been to the doctor the previous day. I can understand how she might want to share the information with her friend, but talking loudly about every detail of it in the middle of the lobby during the noon hour was inappropriate.

You will undoubtedly become friendly with the people you work with and share the details of your life with them. However, there are boundaries, and it is important to recognize what they are because no one may ever think to tell you. You will probably find yourself asking coworkers how their weekend was, about their children, their house, among other things. It's fine to ask someone how they are feeling and to discuss health a bit, but avoid getting into too much detail. Avoid discussing anything that is of a personal nature. Save the private and personal conversations for after hours, away from the office.

Once you feel you have the ability to talk with people and put them at ease, you will undoubtedly feel more comfortable meeting new people. However, even great conversationalists can become tongue-tied when face to face with someone of a higher status, in particular, the boss or head of the company.

Feeling a bit self-conscious or nervous is quite common when talking with a superior, but it doesn't have to be that way. It may help to realize that your supervisor is just as uncomfortable as you are in certain situations. Even the president of a company can feel awkward due to his or her position and may find it difficult to fit in with everyone else.

Show your superiors the same interest and respect you show others. If you find yourself standing or sitting by a superior, use the opportunity to get to know each other better. Don't try to cover big issues or problems in this setting, and definitely don't brag about yourself or complain about the things you don't like.

Gossip is an inevitable part of human interactions, but you are wise to avoid getting involved in discussions about other people. There is little, if any, privacy in most workplaces and chances are your conversation will be overheard. Be cognizant of your surroundings and keep your conversations light and businesslike.

SUMMARY

Remember:

- ✓ Think of your new job as you would a new relationship. Make a commitment to that relationship.

- ✓ Learn to resolve conflict. Don't shy away from or avoid conflict; you can't escape it. Treat problems as an opportunity to grow and learn. Go directly to the source of a conflict and find ways to work through the problems you encounter.

✓ Increase your likeability factor. If you like people and genuinely care about others, chances are they will like you in return. You are likely to attract what you expect, so why not expect the best from others?

✓ Be a breath of fresh air. The exhilaration and anticipation you bring to a new job can be refreshing to those who have lost their zest over the years. Infuse your workplace with your positive energy.

✓ Put things into perspective. Some of the most difficult people and challenging situations can provide you with the most insight.

✓ Learn to solve and resolve problems. Most problems *can* be resolved. Take time to listen to what others are saying. Remember, anytime anyone gives you feedback, whether good or bad, you can learn something of value.

✓ Become a good conversationalist. Get comfortable talking with people at every level, be it your supervisor, coworker, or a customer. Your conversational skills will be an asset for you and a godsend for others.

Chapter 15

Avoiding Potential Pitfalls

MAINTAINING DECORUM IN THE OFFICE

There are expectations in every workplace; some will be clearly communicated while others will not. Every office has its own sense of protocol, and it is important for everyone who works there to understand what's expected. The easiest way to do this is through observation and by asking questions when you are unsure.

Part of your preparation when looking for a job is to research the company and learn about its culture. It is important to not only understand the culture of the organization you work with, but to agree with it—the company's philosophy and manner of doing things. If you are in conflict with the organization's beliefs and values, you will have trouble feeling like you are a part of it.

The way you dress, act, and talk need to blend in with the company culture or you may clash with others. Spend time understanding the culture of the organization in which you work.

Respecting Personal Space

If you step onto an elevator and someone else is already on, it is natural to find a spot that is a comfortable distance away from the other person. If you stand too closely to someone, that person is likely to step back or away from you to maintain a more comfortable distance, which typically is about three to six feet.

At work, your office or cubicle is usually your only personal space. You will make this space more personal by the way you organize it along with the photos, art, and sayings you display. Unless your desk is a total mess, you will probably know if someone has gone through your belongings. If this is done without your permission, you may be offended.

Some people work in very close proximity to others and long for whatever privacy they can get. Be sensitive to that need. Consider the following privacy rules, then do your best to respect the personal space of others:

- Check to be sure it's okay before entering someone's cubicle or office.

- Ask permission before borrowing or using something from a coworker.

- Don't snoop around anyone's office or personal belongings.

- If you need to talk with someone and that person is talking with someone else, either on the phone or in person, don't wait in the doorway—leave and come back when the person is available.

OFFICE GOSSIP

Office gossip is inevitable. Most of the time, what is said has little to do with anything relevant to the work at hand. Gossip of a general nature (vacations, family, and office events) can be enjoyable; "harmful gossip" can be hurtful and is unproductive. Harmful gossip is any information or rumor that demeans the character and reputation of an individual. It is usually disseminated behind the subject's back, which doesn't allow the person a chance to refute or correct the information.

You are bound to hear your fair share of gossip in the workplace. Don't appear too eager to hear or participate in harmful gossip and avoid talking negatively about others. Just because you hear gossip does not mean you have to respond to it.

OFFICE ROMANCES

If you are single, you may meet others you are interested in at work. While some companies have strict policies against employee fraternization, many do not. Know your organization's policy on office dating.

If a relationship evolves naturally, that's fine, but don't try too hard to make something happen. Remember where you are; you are in a place of business, not high school or the college dorm. If you develop a serious relationship with a coworker, be discreet. Refrain from holding hands, kissing, sneaking around, and other obvious displays of affection, and do your best to keep the details of your relationship private. Don't involve others, as it could be especially difficult if the romance doesn't last.

Whatever you do, don't let your relationship—or interest in one—interfere with your work. Be aware that if it becomes common knowledge that you are dating a coworker, your bosses and coworkers will watch both of you more closely. Your relationship could become the subject of harmful gossip, so do what you can to avoid it by conducting yourself in a professional manner at all times.

REPRESENTING YOUR COMPANY PROFESSIONALLY

An activity doesn't have to take place at work to be work-related. Happy hour, lunches, dinners, trade shows, and conventions are just some of the many places where you may find yourself representing your employer. Whether you are talking with someone you met on an airplane, at a party, or a conference, when you are asked what you do, and you reply that you work for a certain company, you are representing that company.

It is important you look and act your best when representing your company at all times. You don't need to be overly cautious, but be aware that what you say and do could be misconstrued or repeated to others and cast you in a bad light.

KNOW YOUR LIMIT

Anytime alcohol is involved, the risk for inappropriate behavior increases. Never feel pressure to drink; in fact, *not* drinking shows considerable restraint and self-control. If alcohol is served and you choose to drink, know your limit and don't overindulge, even if other people are getting drunk. If you lose control, you risk losing your good reputation.

Alcohol and business can be a dangerous mix. Some people have lost their jobs as a result of their drinking or inappropriate behavior, while others have lost even more: the respect of others and their good reputation. Consider the following examples of horrific office party behavior:

- A woman began to tease her boss about his hairpiece and got so drunk she pulled it off of his head!

- Two coworkers disappeared for a few minutes only to be found in an intimate embrace in the women's restroom.

- Two coworkers got into a knockdown, drag-out fight on the dance floor at a holiday party.

An incident that tops all of these stories took place at a company party held at a plush resort. Dinner was served, people were dancing and drinking, and a woman stood up on a table and began to do a striptease—down to her underwear. She was fired the next day.

These are just a few of the many stories I've heard and alcohol played a role in all of them. There is no need to explain why you're not drinking, but you'll have lots of explaining to do if you get drunk and behave inappropriately. If you do decide to drink, sip it slowly and keep your drinking to a minimum.

TO SMOKE OR NOT TO SMOKE?

Smoking is often viewed negatively, and if you smoke, others may think of you less favorably. If you smoke, don't let your smoking interfere with your work or productivity. In addition, make sure you don't reek of smoke. Take your breaks as far away from nonsmokers as possible. If you are required to smoke outside, don't stand in the doorway or in front of the building. This forces everyone who enters the building to inhale your smoke.

Use breath mints frequently and air out your clothes after you've worn them. Even when you can't smell smoke, the scent stays with you.

SOCIALIZING DO'S AND DON'TS

Whether it's a meeting, convention, holiday party, or the company picnic, it helps if you arrive prepared. Knowing the names of people who will be there and having something to talk about will help you interact with others and feel comfortable. Company parties typically include spouses or significant others and it is up to you to help make your guest feel comfortable, too. The following guidelines will help you become a socializing success:

- Introduce yourself to people you do not know.

- Stand as much as possible so that you appear more approachable to others.

- Stay close to your date, especially if he or she has not met your coworkers before.

- Make proper introductions and provide information for the basis of a conversation.

- Stick with light conversational topics.

- Always keep your right hand free (and dry) for a handshake when greeting others.

- Wear a name badge (if provided) on your right side.

- Move around the room rather than plopping yourself down in one spot.

- Mingle and talk with different groups of people.

- Eat before the event to better tolerate alcohol and prevent you from hovering over the buffet table.

- Keep the conversation light—don't engage in gossip or talk about people.

WHAT TO DO IF YOU ARE BEING HARASSED

You should never have to tolerate any form of discrimination or harassment in the workplace or in any other area of your life. Although law does not require them to, most companies have sexual harassment policies. The existence of a policy can help satisfy the courts, which have ruled that appropriate and preventive action in dealing with sexual harassment issues is required. If you are concerned about sexual harassment, find out if your company has a policy and understand its terms.

Companies want their employees to understand the importance of respecting diversity and to behave in a respectful and legal manner. All companies want to avoid negative publicity, which is why it is so important for companies to take a stand of zero tolerance toward harassment and discrimination. Yet, even with the best training in place and a strong stand against inappropriate behavior, incidents can and do happen.

If someone treats you differently than others or consistently acts in a manner that makes you feel uncomfortable, the first thing to do is to approach the person. However, if you truly fear this person or the repercussions of saying something, then it would be wise to go to that person's supervisor or to the human resources department. If you still are not satisfied, you may consider going to the company's legal department.

If you have been involved in a number of incidents, you will want to document them. The more information you have that supports your claim, the better. Try to do everything you can within the company before going outside of the company to file a complaint.

RAISES, PROMOTIONS, AND REVIEWS

I will never forget Bernie, one of my first bosses. Bernie was a nice person, but he never felt comfortable managing people. He just wanted to be everyone's friend. Bernie rarely commented on my job performance, but I sensed he was happy with my effort.

One Friday afternoon before we left for the day Bernie asked me to help him carry some products to the storage room. We were putting away samples, talking and laughing. He said, "You know, Sue, I've never met your parents, but they sure did a good job raising you. You really have a good work ethic." I felt funny inside. It was a little embarrassing to receive a compliment—especially from Bernie. I knew it was hard for him to put into words what he was thinking, and I knew he was doing his best to tell me that he appreciated the work I did.

Everyone wants to be appreciated, and if we fail to get positive feedback from our bosses, we may become insecure about the work we do. But many people are uncomfortable giving out compliments or simply don't know how. It is much easier for some people to tell you what you're not doing or what you're doing wrong than it is to tell you what you are doing right. In fact, some bosses believe that giving a compliment or positive feedback is unnecessary because it is expected that a person will do their job well.

If you find yourself working for someone who is stingy with praise and positive feedback, you may have to find ways to bring praise on yourself. While you don't want to appear needy, there is nothing wrong with checking in with your boss from time to time to inquire how you are doing.

Typically, management will conduct periodic reviews of your development on the job. The length of time between reviews varies from company to company. Participate in your review as much as you can by planning ahead. Compile a list of issues you would like to discuss and don't assume your boss knows everything you do or have done. You may need to remind him or her of the projects you have worked on or the new responsibilities you have mastered since your last review. It also might be useful to create a list of your recent workplace accomplishments for reference during the review.

Reviews are important, and good reviews often lead to a pay raise. If your supervisor doesn't give you either, you may need to request one or the other. I realize that asking for a raise or a review can be difficult, but you need to ask for what you want. No one will look out for you if you don't look out for yourself. Be your own advocate.

When you are having a review it is important to stay calm and to be objective. Determine the action you need to take to improve. Be involved in the discussion as much as possible. Accept any criticism as constructive and avoid the temptation to protect yourself by being too defensive.

CALLING IN SICK

I'd always wondered what would happen if I were sick on a day I was expected to lead a workshop. For years I was able to tell people that I had never cancelled an engagement. I'd given talks and spent days training with the flu, bad colds, and headaches, but always figured that the show must go on and somehow I'd pull through.

Then it happened. I woke up one morning and the room was spinning. I tried to get ready, but became so weak it was impossible. The thought of driving my car to the workshop and then standing and presenting all day made me feel worse.

I called the coordinator of the program and told her that I wouldn't be able to make it. People arrived for the seminar and were sent away. I felt awful thinking about the inconvenience I caused, but there was nothing I could do. I really was ill, and I was heartsick about cancelling. I took solace in the fact that missing the seminar was an anomaly. I knew that no one questioned my motives or integrity. Imagine, however, if I cancelled programs every time I had a headache or a sniffle or I cancelled as many times as I knew it was allowed or until I would likely be reprimanded. That would be wrong. Most companies allow a certain number of sick days, and most managers understand the occasional illness and absence.

If you are frequently sick, even if it is by no fault of your own, you risk being viewed as weak, vulnerable, or undependable. Don't abuse your sick days or claim to be sick when you are not. If you ever do have a prolonged illness or become seriously ill, you will likely find people to be understanding and supportive as long as you haven't created a pattern that has led to mistrust.

Obviously, good attendance is important, but through no fault of your own, you will undoubtedly come down with a cold or the flu at some point in your work life. When you are truly sick, do yourself and everyone else a favor by staying home until you are well. If you are sneezing and coughing, you spread germs to your coworkers. They will not appreciate it if they end up sick because you chose not to stay home.

OWN YOUR POWER

No matter how friendly and easy-going you try to be, you will, undoubtedly, encounter a coworker here and there that gets the best of you. If a coworker has a habit of making remarks that you find degrading, say something. Rather than avoiding the person or becoming stressed every time he or she says something that you feel is offensive, deal with the situation directly by speaking up.

It is difficult to earn the respect of others if you don't respect yourself. By setting boundaries and addressing issues that are important to you, you make a statement about how you feel about yourself. This can be done quietly and politely, and there is no need to put down others in the process. Follow these rules of productive discussion:

- Be direct, but not defensive.
- Be assertive, but not accusatory.
- Be specific, but not nitpicky.

Never allow anyone to have power over you. Own your power.

SUMMARY:

Remember:

- ✓ Respect the personal space of others. Don't take anything from a coworker's desk or enter another employee's cubicle without permission.

✓ Pay attention to the gossip you hear, but don't be the one to spread the news.

✓ Be discreet if you become involved romantically with a coworker.

✓ Represent your company in the most professional manner at all times.

✓ Attend company functions.

✓ Limit your alcohol intake or avoid alcohol altogether at company functions.

✓ Don't let smoking interfere with your work.

✓ Own your power.

Chapter 16

When You're Disappointed and Disillusioned

NOTHING LASTS FOREVER

This book is filled with tips and advice to help you find a job and keep it. However, few jobs provide you with the security of permanent employment. Chances are you will not stay with one company or one position forever. The average person can expect to change careers up to six times over a lifetime. You must prepare yourself to survive and thrive in a changing world.

Even if you do everything right, there is no guarantee your career will be trouble free. Some things will happen that are out of your control, but as long as you are able to respond appropriately, you never have to feel someone else is controlling you or your future.

The key to a successful career is to keep learning, growing, and changing to remain competitive and employable. Continue to network throughout your entire career; your contacts are one of your most valuable resources, and it is easier today than ever before to stay connected. Never expect anyone else to watch out for you or your career—you must watch out for and protect yourself.

Meg worked hard and devoted herself to the company she felt she was a part of. When she learned about impending layoffs throughout the company and in her department, she applied for a different position within her department, confident she would be the one to get the job. She didn't.

Meg's world was turned upside down. Not only did she suddenly find herself unemployed due to the layoff, she also found herself questioning why she didn't get the position she was so qualified for and why her colleagues chose to hire someone out-side of the department instead of her.

Sometimes things happen that catch a person totally off guard. But more often than not, there are subtle signs predicting what's to come. Meg recalled a few minor incidents with a coworker, but she had shrugged them off as insignificant. But those incidents were the reason someone else got the position instead of her.

QUITTING ON A WHIM IS A MISTAKE

The day Thomas found out he was passed over for the promotion he thought was his, he was so upset he quit his job on the spot. It took him many months to find another job, and the one he finally accepted was not as good as the one he left. In retrospect, he regretted leaving so abruptly, but at the time, it seemed like the only thing to do.

When you quit on a whim you are responding to emotion, not logic. Maybe you're offended by something someone said, hurt you didn't get the promotion you expected, or furious to be reprimanded for something you didn't do. You are justified in being upset, but don't allow your emotions to replace reason. Consider the following:

- When you quit on a whim, you may feel relieved at first, but you'll probably feel differently the next day, week, or month when you are sitting home without a job and without a pay-check. Unless you have a backup plan and know how you will survive financially, you may be better off staying until you can be more certain about your future.

- When you quit on a whim you may think you are hurting the organization or the person(s) you are upset with, but you are only hurting yourself. You will be alone, you will be the outcast, and you will be without a job. The suffering you inflict on your-self will be far greater than any suffering you inflict on others.

- When you quit on a whim, you're likely to lose valuable con-tacts. Although you might be able to retain a few contacts, you're bound to lose more than you gain. And you'd better start thinking about what you will tell prospective employers when they ask why (or how) you left and who you'll use as a reference.

- When you quit on a whim, you lose your dignity. When your anger and emotion replace your self-control, you lose more than you gain. You lose your self-respect and the respect of others.

- When you quit on a whim, you're not giving yourself the time you need to make such an important decision. When you give yourself time to think through what happened and how you want to respond, you will arrive at a well thought-out solution with less chance of regret.

WHEN THE TIME HAS COME FOR YOU TO LEAVE YOUR JOB

Leaving a job on good terms benefits both you and your employer. However, it isn't always easy to make that happen. Companies make changes all the time; there are buyouts, mergers, acquisitions, restructuring, and more. You may at some point be laid off or find yourself disillusioned and wanting to leave your job. Or, due to performance or other issues, you may find yourself fired from your job.

According to Marshall Tanick, a lawyer and contributing editor on employment and labor law for *Bench & Bar,* the official magazine of the Minnesota State Bar Association, your employer's ability to fire you depends upon your employment status. People who have employment contracts, are members of labor unions, or work for the government generally cannot be fired unless there is "cause," which means serious misconduct. Most employees don't fit into these categories and are known as "at will" employees. Ordinarily, they can be fired for any reason at the discretion of management, provided that the discharge does not violate a specific law.

If you are let go and you feel your discharge is discriminatory or in violation of some other statute and you make a complaint with the appropriate agency, the employer must be able to show there were legitimate reasons for your dismissal, such as poor work performance, failure to abide by company rules, economic or financial reasons, or any other business-related justification.

No one enjoys being fired or laid off. But if it happens, there is a good chance that you will find another job that will be even better than the one you lost. Change can be positive. When you are hit with unexpected changes, look for the good in what is happening and ways in which you can learn and benefit from the experience.

If you decide to leave a job, it is customary to give an employer a minimum of a two-week notice. This gives you a chance to tie up any loose ends and gives your employer a chance to fill your position and gather any and all necessary information (about the status of ongoing work projects or other work-related issues) from you.

SPEAK UP WHEN YOU LEAVE A JOB

It is fine to notify your employer of your intended departure in writing, but if possible, try to arrange a face-to-face conversation as well. While it is not necessary for you to go into too much detail about why you are leaving, it is always best to give a reason. Common reasons for leaving can be that you are ready for a new challenge, you were offered an exciting new opportunity, or because of your need to earn more money.

I had a conversation with a young woman who told me she had just given notice that she was leaving her job. When I asked her why she was leaving, she told me it was because of her boss, who she felt was treating her unfairly. She said a number of people had recently quit because of this boss.

I asked her if she had told her boss or anyone else the reason for her departure, but she had not. Apparently she was too afraid of this person and assumed no one else would care. So, instead of addressing the real issue, she explained her departure by using the excuse that it was too hard for her to keep up with her schoolwork and her job.

I encouraged her to be honest about her reasons for leaving. How would her boss know there was a problem unless she spoke up? Who was she protecting anyway? While she didn't have to complain or be totally negative, a brief explanation would have been acceptable. If she didn't feel comfortable telling her boss, she could tell her boss's boss, but someone ought to know when there is a specific reason for several people's departure.

WHEN YOU ARE LET GO

If you are ever let go, it can be uncomfortable for you as you work your remaining days on the job. Even though you are on your way out, put your best foot forward because you may cross paths with some of your coworkers or your boss in the future.

I was called in by a company to present a series of seminars to 1,000 employees whose positions were likely to be eliminated. The seminars were necessary because the morale had gotten so low it was unbearable for those who were still working. Some of the people would be staying, some would lose their jobs, and others had plans to work elsewhere. The people who were physically present but emotionally absent were not leaving a very good impression. What many of them failed to realize was that their performance on their way out could impact their future career opportunities.

I realize it is easier said than done to be positive and upbeat when you fear you are losing your job or you actually have lost it, but what choice do you really have? As long as you are employed, work to your potential and be at your best from the first day to the last.

HOW WILL YOU KNOW WHEN IT'S TIME TO GO?

There are many reasons people choose to leave a job. Some people never seem to stay at any job for long, while others never seem to make any changes. There is no right amount of time for you to work at one particular job. While you don't want to become known as a job-hopper or unstable, no one expects you to stay at the same job forever.

Some people stay at a job because the work is easy, others because of the pay and benefits. I'm frequently asked what to do when the passion and enthusiasm for a job is gone but the pay and security make it difficult to leave. If you dread going to work and are not challenged or working to your capacity but sticking around for a paycheck, reconsider. Money is important, but there are many ways to make money. Why not find a job that makes you happy, too?

Any time you find yourself focusing more on what's wrong with your job than on what's good, you ought to reconsider what you are doing and why. Never allow a job to consume you or drain you, and always remain in control of yourself and the direction of your future.

You might consider looking for work elsewhere when:

- You dread going to work each day.

- You think and talk negatively about your job and company.

- You are bored, unchallenged, and not working to your potential.

- You have gone as far as you can go within your company.

- You have been denied your request for a promotion more than three times.

- You cannot remember the last time you received a raise.

- You have complained about things and have not seen any resolution.

- You resent your boss and others in management.

- You don't care any longer about the quality of your work.

- You aren't receiving any positive remarks about your work.

- You are getting complaints about your work or attitude.

- You've outgrown your position.

LEAVING A JOB IN A PROFESSIONAL MANNER

It is important to start a job on a positive note and equally important to end your job positively. Your image and reputation will follow you wherever you go. Whether you are glad or sad to leave your job, do what you can to leave in good standing.

Even when you are down to your last few days of work, keep in mind that you are still working and still being paid. You may be "out of there" emotionally, but physically you are still present and professional behavior is expected at all times.

Some people develop a "who cares" attitude, assuming that they will never see any of their coworkers again, but don't be so sure. The business world is much smaller than it seems, and you are likely to run into people over time. This is why you shouldn't burn any bridges or hurt any relationships. If you do, your behavior may come back to haunt you.

In order to leave a job in a professional manner, do the following:

- Give a minimum of a two-week notice.
- Leave your work area clean and tidy.
- Leave user-friendly information and instructions related to your job.
- Offer to help train your replacement.
- Leave your phone number or e-mail address so others can contact you if necessary.
- Act professionally the entire time of your employment, including the last day.
- Thank everyone who has been helpful to and supportive of you.

EXIT INTERVIEW

Your company may request an exit interview, or you can request one. This gives you the opportunity to bring closure to your departure. If you are asked specific questions about your reasons for leaving, be candid in your responses but not slanderous.

Although I urged the young woman who was leaving because of her boss to state the real reason for her departure, I would never suggest she slander her boss. There are ways to get a point across without sounding bitter and accusatory. If you've never complained before or gone directly to the person with your complaints, it may seem unjustified or unfair. Besides, if you are too negative or angry, not only will your departure be justified, you will be the one who will end up looking poorly.

DIFFICULT SITUATIONS

If you find yourself in a difficult situation, don't despair. Whether your job search is taking longer than expected, you don't get the job you want, or you are passed over for a promotion, you can take action that will help you move forward.

If you aren't sure why you were passed over or didn't get a job, do everything you can to understand what happened. Do a personal assessment and look for the reasons you didn't get the job or promotion you wanted. If you haven't a clue, you may want to ask to find out. Once you know the reason, you can do what's necessary to increase your chances in the future.

You may discover your talents are better suited for another position. Maybe you need to develop proficiency in an area you lack. Perhaps you assumed others knew how much you wanted something, but you failed to make your desires known. Never assume others know what you want.

Be determined to learn from each and every experience, keeping in mind that some of your most difficult incidents will teach you the most. Think about what, if anything, you might have done differently and what you will do in the future. Sometimes the most difficult thing to do after a setback is to simply move on. What happened may be upsetting, but it doesn't have to be; why not assume it happened for a (good) reason? As long as you look for the lessons to be learned from each experience, you will be moving on and in the direction of unlimited possibility and opportunity.

MAKE THE MOST OF YOUR CAREER

Whether you work full time or part time, you will most likely spend more of your time at work than any place else. If you enjoy the work you do, it will be time well spent. However, if you dread the thought of going to work each day, you are simply wasting your time. I can't think of anyone who accepts a job with the intention of becoming disenchanted with it. Yet many people are unhappy and dissatisfied with their jobs and the companies for whom they work.

If you are unhappy, it doesn't have to be that way. Even if you are not yet working in your ideal job or company, you can learn to make the most of each day and feel a sense of satisfaction from the work you do.

Few people start out doing exactly what they dream of. If asked, most people will tell you a thing or two they'd like to change. No workplace is perfect and few jobs are pure enjoyment—it's called "work" for a reason! It's not necessarily the company or job duties that make a job satisfying; more often than not, it's your attitude and perspective that make the difference.

When time flies and you look forward to returning to work each day, you will know you are doing the work you were meant to do. It can take time to find your niche, but you don't have to wait until you do to increase your job satisfaction. The following tips will help you make the most of your career, no matter what stage you are at:

Connect with people. When you connect with people you will find work becomes more enjoyable. Your connection with coworkers can make going to work exciting and positively affect the way you feel about your job. Reach out to others: Say hello and acknowledge the people you see, provide exceptional service, let a coworker know how much you appreciate him or her.

Offer to help someone who is under pressure; be a team player. A job is just a job; it's the people that make a company.

Seek new opportunities both in and outside of work. Sometimes all you have to do is look for new opportunities and they will appear. If you feel stagnant in your job, it may be time to take on a new challenge or additional responsibility. If not at work, consider getting involved in a project outside of work—the satisfaction from working on it may be the thing you need to lift your spirits. Don't expect others to read your mind. Whether you want more responsibility, more pay, or more of a challenge, if you want something, you've got to ask for it, then go for it!

Do more than expected. Feeling down, bored, unchallenged? Maybe you need to pick it up a notch. Empty the trash, make a pot of coffee, offer praise to someone for something he or she has done. Ask a coworker to lunch, beat the deadline, arrive early, leave late. Ask people how they're doing and really listen to what they say. When you do more than what's expected, you'll get more than you expected, too.

Look for the good in your job. When you focus on the good aspects of your job you will stop dwelling on the bad. You already know what you *don't* like about your job. Take some time to identify what you *do* like, no matter how small. Think about what you've learned, challenges you've overcome. Who would you miss seeing day to day if you lost your job tomorrow?

Go job hunting. If you've tried and you cannot find happiness where you are, it may be time to make a change. Look for another job and you might find one—or, you might find that the job you have looks a lot better in comparison.

Some people love every job they have, not because each job is ideal, but because they manage to find something good about each job they have. Although some jobs are better than others, no job will ever satisfy you until you are satisfied with yourself.

SUMMARY

Remember:

- ✔ Look out for yourself: Never rely on anyone else to manage your career.

- ✔ Commit to life-long learning; in order to stay competitive and employed, you must be committed and willing to continually grow and change.

- ✔ Stay connected. Keep in touch with people over the years. Your contacts are one of your most valuable resources.

- ✔ Leave on a positive note. Your last day of a job is as important as your first. Do what you can to leave with your reputation in-tact.

- ✔ Don't quit on a whim. Always take time to think before making a rash, emotional decision.

- ✔ If you are passed over for a promotion, ask why. When you understand what happened, you can do things differently in the future.

- ✔ Learn from your experiences; trying times often teach you the most and can be catalysts for positive change.

- ✔ You'll spend more time at work than anyplace else. Find a job you enjoy or find a way to get more joy out of the job you have.

FURTHER READING AND RESOURCES

The following books and Web sites provide resources and information to help you research, prepare for, and execute your job search. When searching the Web, please keep in mind that URL's often change. If you can't find one of the site's listed below, try using a search engine to locate the organization or resource.

RECOMMENDED READING

Bermont, Todd. *10 Insider Secrets to a Winning Job Search: Everything You Need to Get the Job You Want in 24 Hours-Or Less.* Franklin Lakes, NJ: Career Press, 2004.

Brown, Les. *Live Your Dreams.* New York: Harper Collins, 1994.

Messmer, Max. *Job Hunting for Dummies.* Farmingham, MA: IDG Books, 1999.

Morem, Susan. *How to Gain the Professional Edge, Second Edition: Achieve the Personal and Professional Image You Want.* New York: Checkmark Books, 2005.

Morem, Susan. *101 Tips for Graduates: A Code of Conduct for Success and Happiness in Your Professional Life.* New York: Checkmark Books, 2005.

Nelson, Richard. *What Color Is Your Parachute 2006: A Practical Manual for Job-hunters and Career-Changers.* Berkeley, CA: Ten Speed Press, 2005.

Russell, C.M. *Ultimate Job Hunting Secrets-Essential Tips, Tricks and Tactics for Today's Job Seeker.* Augusta, GA: Morris Publishing 2004.

Strankowski, Donald J. *Get Hired!: 10 Simple Steps for Winning the Job You Desire--in Any Economy.* Lincoln, NE: iUniverse, Inc., 2004.

Tullier, L. Michelle. *The Unofficial Guide to Landing a Job*. Hoboken, NJ: Wiley, 2005.

Vogt, Peter. *Career Wisdom for College Students*. New York: Checkmark Books, 2007.

Yate, Martin. *Knock 'em Dead 2006: The Ultimate Job Seeker's Guide*. Avon, MA: Adams Media, 2005.

CAREER DEVELOPMENT AND JOB SEARCH SITES

America's CareerInfoNet (http://www.acinet.org)

America's JobBank (http://www.ajb.org)

BestJobsUSA (http://www.bestjobsusa.com)

Careerbuilder.com (http://www.careerbuilder.com)

CareerExposure (http://www.careerexposure.com)

CareerLab (http://www.careerlab.com)

Chimby.com (http://www.chimby.com)

CollegeGrad.com (http://www.collegegrad.com)

Collegerecruiter.com (http://www.collegerecruiter.com)

HotJobs.com (http://www.hotjobs.com)

Jobdig.com (http://www.jobdig.com)

Jobhuntersbible.com (http://www.jobhuntersbible.com)

Job-interview.net (http://www.job-interview.net)

Jobweb (http://www.jobweb.com)

Knockemdead.com (http://www.knockemdead.com)

Monster.com (http://www.monster.com)

QuintCareers.com (http://www.quintcareers.com)

SueMorem.com (http://suemorem.com)

Teens4hire.com (http://www.teens4hire.com)

Tipsforgrads.com (http://www.tipsforgrads.com)

Salary.com (http://salary.com)

United States Bureau of Labor Statistics (http://bls.gov/)

Vault.com (http://www.vault.com)

Wageweb.com (http://www/wageweb.com)

WetFeet.com (http://www.wetfeet.com)

Index

A

academic success vs. career success 2
Accountemps (company) 53, 65
alcohol in the workplace 183–184
AllCountryJobs.com (Web site) 44

B

Bench & Bar (magazine) 193
Booz Allen Hamilton (company) 43
Brown, Doug 43

C

career choosing 7–8
  internship as an aid 24–25
  using informational interviews 21–22
career difficulties what to do 198–199
career dissatisfaction what to do 199–201
Career Wisdom for College Students (book) 13, 41
Carnegie, Dale 127–129, 156
changing careers 191–192

chapter summaries 18–19, 26, 36–37, 47, 58–59, 68–69, 92–93, 110–111, 119–120, 131, 146–147, 160–161, 179–180, 189–190, 200
clothing and appearance 73–92
Cober, Rich 43
CollegeRecruiter.com (Web site) 66
commitment to job 163–165
communication skills at work
  good speech attributes 133–134
  managing meetings 145–146
  using the Internet
    e-mail etiquette 142–144
    surfing 144–145
  using the telephone
    answering and placing calls 136–137
    as a business tool 134–135, 138–139
    do's and don'ts 140–141
    pagers and cellular phones 141–142

  speakerphone usage 139–140
  using the "hold" button 135–136
  voicemail 137–138
company parties 185
conversation-making at job
  conversation starters 176–177
  conversation stoppers 177–178
  generating conversation 175
  talking with coworkers 178–179
  talking with supervisors and customers 179
cover letter with resume 55-57
Covey, Stephen 149

D

Dale Carnegie training 27, 28–29
dining manners 109–110
discrimination at a job 186
dress code in the workplace 80–81, 83–84
Dynamic Cover Letters (book) 55

E

educational success
reason for being
hired 3–4
effective meetings, tips
for 145–146
employers on
appearance (survey)
78–79
experience and
internships
reason for being
hired 4

F

favorable impression,
tips for 125–127
finding a job. *See* job
searching
first days of
employment
121–127
*Funk and Wagnalls
New International
Dictionary of the
English Language*
(book) 149

G

goals, setting of 1, 5
Gosyne, Kavita 39

H

habit
definition of 149–
150
Half, Robert 53
handling stress and
conflict 172–175, 189
Hansen, Randall S.
55–56
harassment at a job
186
hard work 1–2

hiring, reasons for
due to educational
success 3–4
due to experience
and internships 4
due to interviewing
skills 4
*How to Win Friends
and Influence People*
(book) 156

I

identifying personal
job skills 8–10
Indeed.com (Web site)
44
Influence, LLC
(marketing agency)
81
informational
interviews 21–24
Internet, using the 44,
142–145
internships 4, 24–26,
28, 41–42
interviewing skills
reason for being
hired 4
interview manners
23–24, 99–100
interviews
after the interview
evaluating 113–114
phone call 116–
117
thank you notes
114–116
at job fairs 107–108
clothing for 79–80,
84–86
during a meal 108–
110
exit protocol 105
first impressions

attitude and body
expression 97–99
good manners 99–
100
voice and expression
95–97
interviewers, survey
of 100–101, 116
phone interview
105–107
preparation for
61–68
presentation during
65–68
questions, asking
and responding to
63–65
researching for
62–63
professional
appearance at
71–92
tips for success
101–105
what to wear at
79–80

J

Jan Stuart Corporation
(business) 81
job
clothing for 80–86,
88–90
commitment to
163–165
company parties 185
conversation starters
176–177
conversation
stoppers 177–178
conversation with
coworkers 178–179

conversation with supervisors and customers 179
developing friendships 175–179
discrimination and harassment 186
generating a conversation 175
leaving a job 191–198
likeability as a success factor 165–168
personal appearance 86–88, 90–92, 122–123
positive attitude as a success factor 169–171
problem solving as a success factor 172–175
raises, promotions, and reviews 186–188
representing your company professionally 183
resolving conflict as a success factor 172–175, 189
respecting yourself 189
responsibilities x
sickness and sick leave 188–189
JOBcentral 2005 Job Seeker Survey 43
job characteristics to consider
hours 17
location 16

organization environment and culture 17–18, 181
salary and benefits 16–17
JobDig.com (Web site) 46
job searching 3, 7–8
accepting a job offer 119
choosing words to describe yourself 13–15
creating a plan 39–40
declining a job offer 119
defining your previous work experience 8–12
job postings and advertisements 4
knowing what you want in a job 15–18
hours 17
location 16
salary and benefits 16–17
work environment and company culture 17–18
myths of 3–4
organizing and following through 46–47
personal contacts and networking 4, 47
process of looking 29–36
avoiding distractions 31–32
establishing a routine 30–31

expanding personal knowledge 32–33
importance of patience 35–36
improving your presentation 34–35
using your network 33–34
references 57
rejection, dealing with and learning from 118–119, 198
selling yourself 12–15
utilizing resources
career and job fairs 43–44
career centers 42
company contacts 43
company Web sites 43
employment agencies 45
the Internet 44
internships 41–42
personal contacts 41, 47
professional associations 45
waiting for job offer 117–118
want ads 27–28, 45–46

K
Kaminer, Craig 81–82
Knock 'Em Dead (book series) 65

L
LaFrance, Marianne 90

leaving a job
  being fired 193–195
  exit interview 197–198
  giving notice and speaking up 194–195
  knowing when to leave 195–196
  leaving in a professional manner 195, 197
  quitting on a whim, reasons against 192–193
LinkedIn.com (Web site) 44
Lipe, Jay 22

M
Mackes, Marilyn 78
maintaining good (working) relationships, tips for 173–175
managing meetings 145–146
The Marketing Toolkit for Growing Businesses (book) 22
Messmer, Max 65
Minnesota State Bar Association 193

N
NACE. See National Association of Colleges and Employers
National Association of Colleges and Employers (NACE) 41–42, 78

Nelson, Bob 155
networking 4, 21, 25, 33–34, 45, 191

O
office. See workplace
OfficeTeam (company) 77
1001 Ways to Reward Employees (book) 155

P
personal adornments 73, 79, 86–87
personal commitment to job 163–165
personal contacts, importance of
  in job searching 4, 21–23, 25, 41
personal experiences aid in defining self 10–12
personal hygiene 87–88
personal image improvement 72–78
personal job skills, identifying 8–10
Procter & Gamble (business) 90
professional appearance
  at work 80–86, 121–127
  importance of 71–92, 122–124
  potential barriers to 86–88
Professional Image Institute 71

R
raises, promotions, and job reviews 186–188
relationships
  likeability factor 165–167
  negative vs. positive attitudes 168–172
  stress and conflict resolution 172–175, 189
  with coworkers 175–179
  with people 163–175
  resolving conflicts, tips for 173–175
resume
  common mistakes 51–52
  cover letter with common mistakes 56
  importance of 55
  what to say 56–57
  creating 49–51
  presentation of 53–55
  proofreading of 52–53
  style of 50–52
  telephone follow up 57–58
  what to include 49
Resume Magic: Trade Secrets of a Professional Resume Writer (book) 51
Rothberg, Steven 66
Russell, Bill 66–67
Russell, Chris 44

S

Secrets of the Job Hunt
(blog) 44
setting goals,
importance of 1, 5
*Seven Habits of Highly
Effective People* (book)
149
sickness and sick leave
from a job 188–189
smoking in the
workplace 184–185
success
and luck 4–5
attitude, importance
of 3
dependability,
importance of 2–3
learning from
difficulties 171–172
likeability as a factor
165–168
myths of 1–5
positive attitude as a
factor 169–171
problem solving as a
factor 172–175
resolving conflict as a
factor 172–175
truths about 1–5
success and habits
attitude improvement
151–152
being a team player
153–154
consideration and
respect for others
157–159
generating
enthusiasm 150–
151
keeping your word
157

positive
reinforcement for
others 155–156
proactive behavior
154–155
punctuality 156–157
self-promotion 159–
160
standing up for
yourself 152–153
success factors in a job
likeability 165–168
positive attitude
169–171
problem solving
172–175
resolving conflict
172–175
survey of employers on
appearance 78–79
surveys of interviewers
100–101, 116

T

Tanick, Marshall 193
tips
for a favorable
impression in the
workplace 125–127
for effective meetings
145–146
for good dining
manners 109–110
for handling conflict
and maintaining
good relationships
173–175
for resolving conflicts
173–175
for success at
interviews 101–105

U

using the Internet
at the office 142–145
for job searching 44

V

Vault.com (Web site)
99, 116
Vogt, Peter 13, 24, 41

W

Whitcomb, Susan
Britton 51–52
work communication
skills. *See*
communication skills
at work
work experience before
job searching 8–10
workplace
and alcohol 183–184
and smoking 184–
185
clothing
recommendations
80–86, 88–90
communication skills
133–146
company parties 185
discrimination at
186
dress code 80–81,
83–84
employer
expectations 127–
128
employer fears 129–
130
facial hair 91
first days of
employment 121–
127
hair styling 90–91

hands 92
harassment at 186
maintaining decorum
  181
new employee
  expectations 127–
  128
office gossip 182
office romances
  182–183

professional
  appearance 121–123
professional behavior
  123–127
respecting personal
  space 181–182
respecting yourself
  189
socializing do's and
  don'ts 185

tips for a favorable
  impression 125–
  127

Y
Yale University 90
Yate, Martin 65
young adults today,
  characteristics of xi